Pre-Accident Investigation Media

The

Principles of Human Performance

A contemporary update
of the building blocks of Human Performance
for the new view of safety.

Copyright

The 5 Principles of Human Performance:
A contemporary update of the building blocks of Human
Performance for the new view of safety
Author: Todd E. Conklin, Ph.D.

© 2019, Todd E. Conklin

PreAccident Media

Santa Fe, New Mexico

Other Books by Todd Conklin

"Simple Revolutionary Acts: Ideas to Revitalize Yourself and Your Workplace." 2004.

"Pre-Accident Investigations: An Introduction to Organizational Safety." 2012.

"Pre-Accident Investigations: Better Questions – An Applied Approach to Operational Learning." 2016.

"Workplace Fatalities: Failure to Predict – A New Safety Discussion on Fatality and Serious Event Reduction." 2017.

Dedication

This book is for all the folks who have had to face a room full of people who don't believe they need to change the way they think. Nothing is as difficult as a person who believes they already know the answer – when you are not certain you know the question.

Get caught doing the right thing.

Thanks to Jeff Segler, Howard Nekimken, and Leslie Hinton.

Table of contents

Preface

There is nothing new here. The struggles we fight have been fought before. The need for a better approach to understanding how work is conducted and how workers are expected to adapt and be productive did not start with the introduction of Human Performance philosophies 30 years ago. Humans have long struggled with justice and judgement, the strong and powerful class of people versus the strong and adaptive class of people. One group has power the other group has knowledge. It didn't start with Frederick Taylor and his struggle with this, and most it likely will not end with us. We won't solve the problems of inequality between the powerful and the powerless.

As I write this book, my country has started separating children from their parents on the southern border. This horrible act is being done to deter people from other countries, mostly Central and South American countries, from immigrating to the United States. I am disgusted by all of this. There will never be a time in our history where people will look back at the practice of taking young children away from their parents as a point of honor or improvement. No one in the future will claim this was an effective deterrent, or that separating children from their parents made America better. Separating children from parents to deter immigration is a ridiculous idea that is being done for senseless reasons.

Sadly, the separation of children in order to amplify some "larger social accountability message" is not a unique event in the history of the world

1

nor are horrible acts committed against families new. Separating children from parents is not even a unique event in the history of the US. Sadly, we as a society have done horrible things before and I am afraid if we don't learn from this we may do horrible things again.

Why won't virtuous and smart people stop this insanity? What is stopping people from seeing the separation of immigrant children from their parents as profoundly evil and morally wrong?

Oscar Wilde, while in prison, wrote a letter to the editor of the British newspaper the Daily Chronical in 1897 and discussed this separation of children from their parents as a deterrent to, in this case, crime in England. It's inexplicable that his words written so long ago still apply to current issues at the United States border. Moreover, Wilde's words have much to say about our discussion (and work) of workplace safety and reliability issues in all our organizations.

Here are two excerpts of what Oscar Wilde wrote in 1897:

> "The cruelty that is practiced by day and night on children in English prisons is incredible, *except to those that have witnessed it.*
>
> "Wherever there is centralization there is stupidity. What is inhuman in modern life is officialism. Authority is as destructive to those who exercise it as it is to those upon whom it is exercised. The people who uphold the prison system have excellent

intentions. Those who carry it out are human in intention also. Responsibility is shifted onto the disciplinary regulations. It is supposed that because a thing is s rule it is right. *It is not the prisoners who need reformation, it is the prison.*"

I agonized about including this Wilde quote and this discussion of the actions taken on the US border in 2018 in the introduction to this book. I worried that writing about this great injustice would take the messages from this book and misdirect the reader into some type of social argument, a notion of context and extremes, neither simply understood. Some agree with my feelings, while others may disagree. There is the potential to lose the power of our message on reliability by mixing the message regarding social and moral actions.

Then I read the two lines in \Oscar Wilde's quote.

"Cruelty…is incredible…, except to those that have witnessed it."

"It is not the prisoners who need reformation it is the prison."

The profound ideas Wilde uses to begin and close his thoughts in this letter says much to us about our world today. When we live within our organizations we don't easily see the incredible. Wilde goes on to suggest the idea our organizations won't be better off by fixing the people. We will better off by fixing the organization. A rule is not righteous simply because it's a rule.

It's not workers who need reformation, it is the workplace. It's not our leaders that need reformation, it's the leadership system we utilize. If you place good people into bad systems, you will undoubtedly get undesired outcomes. We've all known this to be true for a long time.

The pressure to focus on blame and not fix systems and processes is the battle we fight when conducting work. We are constantly reminding our workplaces that knowing **what** failed will better help us fix problems in an effective and sustainable way and knowing **who** failed nonproductively focuses on blame. Knowing who failed assumes adverse intent and assumes holding someone accountable will deter others from having harmful intentions. That is not true at the US border nor in our organizations and systems.

We are lucky that great people with great intentions are a part of our newly enlightened systems; perhaps we should take time to understand that systems matters. Rules are not suitable simply because they are rules. People don't have negative intentions because they intend to produce undesirable outcomes. Bad outcomes are a product of weak and brittle systems, not weak and brittle people.

One of the most important things we can do is to keep the discussion of the Principles of Human Performance active. The principles are our building blocks of what we know are true. Wilde said, "It is not the prisoners who need reform, it is the prison." I would capture Wilde's idea and modernize it to say, "it is not our workers and operators who need fixing, it is our workplaces."

I hope you like this book.

Pre-Accident Investigation Media...

The 5 Principles of Human Performance:

A contemporary update
of the building blocks of Human Performance
for the New View of safety.

5

Chapter One

It Begins...

I was at a meeting several months ago that was put together by Todd Hohn. Todd is really good about getting interesting groups of people together to address severe safety problems, and this meeting was talking about the most dreadful problem of all, fatal events. As a part of the meeting, each person gave a short presentation to tell the rest of the group where their organization was on the journey to prevent fatalities. It was an excellent meeting; a great deal was learned and shared.

Charles Major and Wes Harvard were a part of this meeting and when it came time for them to present, they produced a chart that was probably 7 feet tall. Charles and Wes are long-time human performance programmatic managers for a large utility company. Charles and Wes both know a lot about Human Performance and they have learned how to give life to Human Performance in an organization that is working hard to be robust and resilient. They both teach Human Performance worldwide. Wes began their presentation by asking an important question, "What is Human Performance and what is it we represent? There are a ton of good ideas out there in the world of Human Performance, what are our core principles? What is it that makes up the foundation of Human Performance?"

I was surprised by their questions. I had always assumed that the 5 principles from the INPO/DOE[1] handbook would be the 5 principles that we would all be utilizing. I realized at that time that these principles had morphed and changed, and that some organizations had simply stopped discussing any of the principles at all. Human Performance was becoming whatever an organization needed it to be. Don't get me wrong, I am not really a purist and I am certain the ability for Human Performance to morph and change is not all bad, but the principles have always seemed to ring true and are the foundation upon which we built Human Performance approaches and the associated materials. I built my fundamentals training class around those classic 5 principles. I thought they were an extremely important and illuminating part of the philosophical change in thinking Human Performance helps an organization create.

This all caused me to think back a bit farther. About a year ago, Bob Edwards said something interesting to me in a conversation about this very topic. If you haven't met Bob Edwards, you should, he is one of the foremost experts on operational learning, using the Learning Team concept, in the world. Bob goes all over working with companies to get them to talk to their workers, and he is effective at it. At the time, Bob's comment didn't seem to be too important, but now considering what Charles and Wes had just presented, Bob's comment seemed really important. Bob said to me, "Human

---

[1] I have not defined these terms/acronyms in the introduction in order to promote further discussion of both the INPO and the USDOE Handbooks for Human Performance. These documents are discussed in greater detail later on in this book.

Performance is like a religion without a bible." We have all the components of a revolutionary movement based upon belief, what we lack is the driver for our faith, a document that tells the world what we believe. Suddenly, the 5 principles are starting to feel even more important. At the same time, I realized that most of the other Human Performance classes taught in my current organization lacked any kind of discussion around the Principles of Human Performance, which seemed strange. Remember, I used the 5 Principles of Human Performance as the organizing principle for my entire class.

So, What is a Principle?

No person is perfect. No matter how much experience, practice, and attention a worker gives a task, there will always be the potential for that person to make a mistake. Therefore, the statement "human beings are not able to perform tasks perfectly every time" is always true. Human imperfection, therefore, would be a principle about how humans perform work.

Basic truths are called principles. Principles are defined as a list of fundamental truths or propositions that serve as the foundation for a system of beliefs or behaviors. A principle is dependable and predictable. An organization can utilize these principles to build and maintain systems, processes, and the organization itself within which work is being accomplished. Human Performance Principles are building blocks whose points we know are true and make up the foundational thinking of safety and reliability philosophy.

Because we know these principles, we can use the fundamental knowledge of these principles to both predict and improve our organizations. A principle allows us to design organizations where we can predict, determine, and formulate the future performance of individual actors in our organizations.

Just as there are some basic principles of physics that guide the universe, there are some basic principles that guide organizational reliability. Like gravity, principles are powerful and like for law, principles must be followed. In the workplace, a principle is like a guide, or a predictor of what can be avoided in the future of our organizations. Principles matter because they help us unify our understanding of what is always true in our organizations. From that unification, our organizations can bring some certainty into an uncertain world.

The basic foundation of Human Performance Improvement is not to be a model as part of a program. The basic foundation of Human Performance is a set of principles that represent some basic truths around how humans will perform (or will not perform) within our organization. These principles represent a philosophical shift away from traditional thinking about how people behave in organizations towards contemporary thinking about how our organizations function best with the workers in the organization.

I must admit, I wish there were a model that we could use to describe this change from the traditional safety and reliability methodologies to the more enlightened "safety differently" approach that is so foundational to Human Performance. Having a model seems easier to communicate throughout the community of practitioners. A model would be easy to explain and would be seductive. A model would allow us to say to our organization's members, "do these six things and we will be better, safer, and more reliable." Unfortunately, the world is not that simple.

The idea that principles have influence and power over how management philosophies are used in creating organizational improvement is not new; leadership and management principles have been around for hundreds of years. W. Edwards Deming's 14 Points come to mind as an excellent example. Deming was a mathematical physicist

Deming's 14 Points	
1. Create constancy of purpose	8. Drive out fear
2. Adopt the "New" philosophy	9. Break down barriers
3. Cease dependence on inspection and audits	10. Eliminate slogans like zero defects or accidents
4. End "lowest" bid contracts	11. Eliminate targets and goals
5. Constantly learn and improve your system	12. Remove barriers that rob workers for pride of expertise
6. Institute on the job training	13. Institute education and learning
7. Create an environment where Supervision can succeed	14. Transformations is everyone is the job of in the Organization

who became the father of the modern quality movement. I see a lot of similarities between the improved quality journey that organizations undertook 25 years ago and the Human Performance journey organizations are now undertaking. Deming's thought system he called the "System of Profound Knowledge," includes four components or "lenses" through which to view the world (see if you notice any similarities):

1. System Appreciation;

2. Understanding Variability;

3. Human Psychology; and finally,

4. The Value of Learning.[2]

Deming presented his 14 points as practices that should be followed. However, Deming continued to edit and clarify these points in his seminars and writings throughout the rest of his career. Principles are constantly being updated, which is a normal outcome for a philosophy that emphasizes continuous learning and improvement. The knowledge that even Deming "tweaked" his 14 Points started me thinking.

How the New View Rejuvenated the Original Human Performance Principles

We have momentum for improvement, but we have not codified our building blocks of Human Performance. We have not sufficiently emphasized the importance of the principles, the basic truths that make up the philosophy of Human Performance. We had not been having this principle discussion but suddenly, Charles' and Wes's 7-foot list of what we believe became fascinating to me at a level I had not thought of before. Here is the list of the Human Performance

---

[2] Deming, W. Edwards. 1986. *Out of the crisis*. Cambridge, Mass: Massachusetts Institute of Technology, Center for Advanced Engineering Study.

Principles that Wes has collected over the years from peers, leaders, academics, practitioners, and friends. I am not sure any of these are wrong, but I am also fairly sure that many of these would not qualify as principles, fundamental building blocks of Human Performance.

Here is the exact list of all the principles that Charles' and Wes' had collected and presented that day:

- People want to do a good job
- People are fallible and even our best make mistakes... and take risks and drift
- Error likely situations are predictable, manageable and preventable
- People achieve high levels of performance due largely to reinforcement and encouragement from peers, leaders, and subordinates
- Individual behaviors are influenced by organizational processes and values
- All behaviors are heavily influenced
- Context drives behaviors
- People do what makes sense to them...at that moment...in the context of the work...that we helped them create
- Our organization is precisely tuned to get the behavior that it gets
- Events can be prevented... when we choose to learn from events we can improve
- 90% of our events are caused by something other than just the individual

- People are as safe as they need to be without being overly safe in order to get work done
- Blame is the enemy of understanding
- Learn, or fail...again
- We can learn and improve or blame and punish, but you can't do both
- Safety is not the absence of an accident, but is the presence of capacity
- Success comes from making it easy to do the right thing and hard to do the wrong thing
- Your reaction matters
- Learning is vital
- Blame fixes nothing
- Understanding how and why mistakes occur and applying lessons learned can reduce incidents
- Majority of errors associated with incidents stem from latent conditions rather than active errors
- Violations (of rules and procedures) are rarely malicious, but well-meaning behaviors intended to get the job done
- Safety as a capacity in organizational excellence
- Successful outcomes result from what you do and not implied by an absence of negative outcomes
- Learning is vital to building capacity

What do you think? What would you add to this list? Although massive, the list is by far incomplete.

All of these would be good discussion topics, all of these would make a pretty interesting book. All of them are certainly reflective of

Human Performance philosophies and fundamentals. Some of these feel like folklore and some I wish I would have thought of myself. The biggest problem is there are too many.

Perhaps we could start to bin these "principles" into categories in an attempt to refine this list. That is how it began. I pondered these principles and came back to the original 5 Principles of Human Performance from the INPO/DOE handbook. It seemed that the long list of principles from Charles and Wes were mainly captured in INPO/DOE list.

It looks like the original 5 Principles of Human Performance were written to be directed toward the worker. I knew this was not correct, human performance is not a philosophy that changes the worker's behavior, Human Performance represents a philosophical change in the way we define and manage safety. The Principles of Human Performance are really much more directed at the organization's leaders, not the organization's workers and operators.

What to Understand About Human Performance?

Human Performance is not done to the worker (fix the worker), therefore Human Performance doesn't utilize that approach to manage organizational safety and reliability. Human Performance doesn't offer one approach or method for implementation. There is no such thing as Human Performance done correctly or for that matter incorrectly. Human Performance is a philosophical shift in how you manage safety, production, and reliability. What Human

Performance offers is a set of principles, a set of building blocks that don't really tell an organization what to do, but rather help an organization know what to avoid (what *not* to do). Principles are like truths, they are an accurate way to determine the foundational premises of our thinking. "We don't know everything, but we know these 5 Principles of Human Performance seem to be consistently woven throughout all of our thinking, learning, and actions in order to create deliberate operational stability, reliability, and improvement."

The original 5 principles were directed at the workforce, those principle were being "done to the worker." The original Human Performance Principles was worker-centric and crafted our understanding of safety within the "old view" paradigm. If INPO/DOE wrote the 5 Principles of Human Performance now, I feel certain these principles would encompass a much stronger leader-centric approach. Perhaps, all we needed to do was to take the original 5 Principles of Human Performance and view them through the lens of what is being affectionately called "Safety Differently" or the New View of safety. In essence, what we need to do is update the original 5 principles using what we have learned about the New View of safety, not really change the principles. The principles have stood the test of time and have aged well.

Clarity creeped into my thinking. The problem was not the principles, the issue was we defined safety success 25 years ago as the reduction of failure. The old definition of safety was the absence of accidents and injuries. It would make sense that the 5 Principles of Human

Performance would therefore be directed at workers, "know these 5 things and you will have fewer accidents." If the goal was to reduce failure, it would go without saying the principles would focus on eliminating negative outcomes.

Understanding the original principles through the lens of the new safety philosophy may be the filter we need to seize this new way of thinking and reestablish our 5 Principles of Human Performance in an enhanced, more contemporary manner. To do this, we should discuss the "Safety Differently" approach.

Core Ideas of Safety Differently

When Sidney Dekker coined the phrase "Safety Differently" late one night, he must have been looking for a means to motivate readers to switch approaches from the very ingrained old view of safety and reliability to the New View of safety, reliability, and capacity. Dekker had been looking for a way to shift thinking from old principles of safety, preventing bad things from occurring, to new principles, ensuring positive outcomes. Dekker wanted leaders, workers and operators in their organizations to view the world in a way that was different than the traditional way organizational leaders, workers, and operators had been taught. The initial quest was to change the way we defined safety success and to change the way we viewed workers. Safety was no longer the absence of accidents and workers were no longer a problem to be fixed.

This New View of safety is thoughtfully built around four distinct ideas. Ideas that represent a much different way to think about safety. These four ideas represent the Principles of Safety Differently.

Traditional Safety	Safety Differently
1. Workers are the problem to be fixed. We fix safety by making workers better.	1. Workers are not the problem – They are the problem solvers.
2. We must tell workers what to do and, perhaps more importantly, not to do.	2. We don't tell our organizations what to do – ask them what they need.
3. Safety is the absence of accidents.	3. Safety is not the absence of accidents – it is the presence of capacity.

In order to define the Principles of Human Performance we will first need to introduce the Principles of Safety Differently.

First, the New View of safety changes the definition of success. Safety is not the absence of accidents, safety is the presence of capacity. We don't improve safety by eliminating bad things, we make safety better by improving our systems, processes, planning, and operations.

Secondly, we have to change the way we view our workers. Traditional safety saw workers as problems to be fixed. That is why we have had so many programs that track worker behavior. For a long time, we thought the problem was our mistake prone and uncontrolled workforce. If we wanted safety to improve, we would simply needed to fix each worker, one at a time, until all workers conducted work safely.

The Safety Differently approach views workers and operators not as problems, but as problem solvers. Smart and adaptive workers who understand the organization and the organization's systems and processes can be invited to help identify and solve the multitude of safety issues that exist within the organization. Once workers are engaged, they become the experts in how work should be conducted safely and effectively.

Thirdly, we would constrain workers, telling them what to do or, more often, what not to do. Under the newly recognized expertise the workers bring to both problem identification and solution generation, instead of constraining workers, we ask that what they need in order to be successful in conducting their work. They tell us and we listen and provide the support and shared accountability for accomplishing successful work.

Lastly, with a new definition of safety success and a new way to view workers and operators, we realize that we can manage failure better by understanding success. Where we previously tried to prevent bad outcomes from occurring (which was like playing a giant game of whack-a-mole), now we actually spend our time and energy ensuring that the correct things, controls, people, and processes continue to be present and in place. We discovered a way to manage failure by understanding normal, successful work. After all, your organization is successful much more often than unsuccessful. Failure is rare and success is normal.

This New View gave us a set of principles for Safety Differently that we could use to refocus the 5 Principles of Human Performance. The once murky understanding of these principles, including Wes' giant list of principles started to become more and more distinct. We didn't need new principles, what we needed was to help understand our original principles in a fresh way. We were revitalizing and rejuvenating the 5 Principles of Human Performance.

Here are the 4 Principles of Safety Differently that I used to begin the process of refocusing and understanding the 5 Principles Human Performance:

The 4 Principles of Safety Differently

1. Safety is not defined by the absence of accidents, but by the presence of capacity.
2. Workers aren't the problem, workers are the problem solvers.
3. We don't constrain workers in order to create safety, we ask workers what they need to do work safety, reliably, and productively.
4. Safety doesn't prevent bad things from happening, safety ensures good things happen while workers do work in complex and adaptive work environments.[3]

---

[3] These are in no way "official" principles – but more an observation of what I have observed as some important tenants of this New View of workplace safety.

I can't begin to tell you how much this helped my understanding of why the principles had not sustained themselves over the last dozen or so years. I knew the principles had the right framework, they were thoughtful, tested, and came from theories of great intellectuals and scholars. I know these principles have succeeded in improving organizations I have helped. The 5 Principles of Human Performance didn't get less valuable, the way we now think about safety represents a complete turnaround. The principles are robust, as long as you view them through the 4 Principles of Safety Differently.

Look at the 5 Principles for Human Performance now, directly on the heels of just reading the 4 Principles of Safety Differently and determine if these exhibit renewed energy and substance. In fact, let me place them next to each other to demonstrate that the 4 Principles of Safety Differently give a sharper meaning to the 5 Principles of Human Performance.

The 4 Principles of Safety Differently

1. Safety is not defined by the absence of accidents, but by the presence of capacity.
2. Workers aren't the problem, workers are the problem solvers.
3. We don't constrain workers in order to create safety, we ask workers what they need to do work safety, reliably, and productively.
4. Safety doesn't prevent bad things from happening, safety ensures good things happen while workers do work in complex and adaptive work environments.

And

The 5 Principles of Human Performance

1. Error is normal. Even the best people make mistakes.
2. Blame fixes nothing.
3. Learning and Improving are vital. Learning is deliberate.
4. Context influences behavior. Systems drive outcomes.
5. How you respond to failure matters. How leaders act and respond counts.

The Discussion

This book will look at the 5 Principles of Human Performance principle by principle, chapter by chapter. I will engage in a longer discussion about each of the principles. These are principles, the building blocks of Human Performance, through which we have established a new way to think about safety and reliability in our organizations. I would like to submit early on in our discussion that I am not an expert, I have no more knowledge than other people have about Human Performance. If I have one advantage it would be that I have been working with these ideas for a long time with many different organizations. I don't promise to be right (whatever that is), but I do promise to create an opportunity for all of us to thoughtfully explore the 5 Principles of Human Performance, one principle at a time.

I am sure this will not be the final version. I don't want these discussions to be final versions, I would like to use this book as a starting point of many more discussions and books to come. Let's see what you think and what you can add to these ideas. Jump in! There's plenty of room.

Chapter Two

Principle Number One

People Make Mistakes

- Errors are normal.
- What is error?
- Since error is a normal part of human existence, error is never causal.
- Error is not the opposite of success. Error is a part of being successful.
- Error exists in success as well as failure.
- Errors are not choices. Error only becomes a choice in retrospect.
- You can't remove error, so you must defend against the inevitability of error.
- Good systems build in error tolerance. Knowing errors will happen is a good thing.
- Error without significant consequence is the closest thing to "leading indicator" data.

People are fallible, and even the best people make mistakes.

Error is universal. No one is immune regardless of age, experience, or educational level. The saying, "to err is human," is indeed a truism. It is human nature to be imprecise—to err. Consequently, errors will occur. No amount of counseling, training, or motivation can alter a person's fallibility. Dr. James

Reason, author of *Human Error* (1990) wrote: *It is crucial that personnel and particularly their managers become more aware of the human potential for errors, the task, workplace, and organizational factors that shape their likelihood and their consequences. Understanding how and why unsafe acts occur is the essential first step in effective error management.* [4]

Humans: An Incredibly Adaptive and Creative Group of Problem Solvers

Human beings are amazing. Have you really thought much about how amazing your workers truly are? You are surrounded by these creative and adaptive people every day. Your workers are constantly solving problems and adjusting operations while at the same planning birthday parties and picnics. Your organization relies upon adaptive and creative workers to survive and thrive in your current market. Robots are great, but can a robot remember that when you hear that high-pitched whirl on press number three it means that you have 2 hours to replace the spool, but not with the green one, that one never works correctly. It is hard to accurately reflect how much you count on creative, adaptive, and agile workers to keep operations humming along, but you count on these adaptive and creative workers a lot, much more than you think. Creative, adaptive, smart, and experienced workers keep the normal variability of your operations in check ALL THE TIME.

---

[4] Excerpt taken from the DOE Standard, Human Performance Improvement Handbook, Volume 1. Concepts and Standards, DOE-HDBK-1028-2009 June 2009.

The problem is with all of that creativity and adaptability comes a lot of excess human "baggage." People are complicated and multi-dimensional. People have emotions and physical needs. People get tired. People get tired and cranky. Your workers are amazing, but they're not machines and they will never ever have machine reliability. People don't obey the laws of physics very well, but they do obey the laws of physiology. I once had a rather famous physicist at Los Alamos National Laboratory tell me in quite an exasperated tone, "Physics is easy – people make my job hard" and he was completely serious when he said it.

Human workers are the most important part of your production operations, whereas they are also the least reliable part of your system. Workers are amazing at handling variability, they just can't reliably handle boredom and repetition; they hate inefficiencies, and they get offended by overly invasive supervision. Workers can fix giant operational problems in real-time and still trip on the concrete floor of your plant. Workers are smart enough to know how to adjust a machine to maximize production when influenced by all types of variabilities, yet not smart enough to avoid stabbing their own hand with a razor knife. That's what being human is like, just one damn thing after another.

This is what we have in our workplaces. We rely on these adaptive, but unreliable people to produce successful work. Normally, this relationship between fallible human and complicated system works quite well, until it does not work well. Not everything goes right, and it is at these times that we must seek to understand the first principle of Human Performance – People make mistakes.

Humans: Inherently inconsistent and unreliable

People are exceptional problem solvers, but are not exceptionally reliable. People can solve complex problems quickly, but do not always get it right. Knowing that people are mistake-prone machines is not shocking or bad news for your organization. In fact, knowing that people make mistakes and errors is actually quite enlightening and helpful; I think this knowledge is quite liberating. We now know we should not build systems that expect perfection from our human operators. We do not have perfect operators and we know that going in. The problem is, we **do** build systems that expect perfection from our human operators and we are very often surprised and shocked by the fact our workers are not perfect; and we do it all the time. When will we learn?

Systems that are designed with the belief that the human operator will be perfect are not your worker's fault; the workers you have working for you never promised perfection and these same workers have very little control over the systems and processes that you hand over to them in the name of managing production efficiently. Building a system that has as its only line of defense the need for perfect operations every time the system is operated is a poorly conceived and poorly designed system. That failure is the organization's liability and should not be directed at the individuals of the organization. You can never blame people for not being perfect because people never promised they would or could be perfect. Planners, managers, and designers make two enormous assumptions. The first assumption is that every day is the same and that process variability will be identified and driven out of the work before the worker starts their tasks. The second assumption is that the worker will perform consistently and perfectly every time the work is done; the mistaken belief that the worker will exhibit machine reliability.

Knowing that human beings are inherently inconsistent and unreliable is helpful in creating and planning your organization's systems and processes. It's funny, you would think calling your workforce inconsistent and unreliable would be a bad thing, and yet it is not a bad thing at all. You don't design expectant PERFECT operations, you now have permission (and knowledge!) to design a system that expects IMPERFECT operations and has the ability to tolerate a bored, a sleepy, or hungry worker, and not fail in some catastrophic manner.

Everybody Makes Mistakes

Here is what we know for sure; error is universal. Everyone makes errors. Even your very best worker on his or her very best day will make a mistake.

Perhaps more importantly, what the first principle of Human Performance best illuminates is error is normal and therefore our organizational expectations must reflect this reality. Everyone makes errors, so therefore errors are a normal function of being a human being. Asking people to not make errors is not an effective strategy. Error is normal, which means in many ways error is not very interesting as a failure causal factor. Error is normal and because it is normal it can never be considered a special case, an unusual outcome, or an unexpected event. You should expect error; you should have seen it coming.

If everyone makes mistakes and human error is normal, then the premise is if you design and create a process that demands perfection from an imperfect and normal human operator *and* your designed process fails because of an operator error or mistake, *this failure is the product of the system design and not of the human operator*. As attractive as it is to say human error is special and unique in our systems, the bottom line is that human error is neither special nor unique; human error is normal and people make mistakes. It is the difference between the idea that the worker failed the system (old view) or the system failed the organization (new view). There will be more about this when we talk about blame. Blame makes errors less like errors and more like choices, and errors are never choices; you'll see this in the next chapter.

For years we used a data set in Human Performance classes to explain and quantify human error that came from quality programs in manufacturing facilities. We would say the average worker or operator makes between 5 to 7 errors per hour. I have no idea if this number is correct. The number could be high or it could be low. I have long been convinced the error-rate number we used for all those years in our Fundamentals of Human Performance Class is made up

28

as I can't really find a source for that number in any academic publication. It makes for a good story, but I am just not certain the number is accurate.

As attractive as it is to be able to quantify error rates, even the idea of finding the number of errors per hour seems to attach error to workers as if the workers would have some type of control over making or not making the error. You know how this would go; we would start to measure errors per hour and then ask people to reduce their number from 5 to 7 errors per hour down to 3 to 5 per hour. We might even put some financial incentives in our program to reduce the error number even lower. I think talking about the number of errors made per hour sends the wrong message at several levels. It makes errors look like they are within the workers span of control. If the worker would try harder, the worker would make less errors. Errors are normal, people make mistakes, trying not to make an error probably makes it more likely that you will make the very error you're trying to avoid. Error represents a vicious circle which takes us right back to the first principle, people make mistakes.

Instead, I have become interested in attaching error to two distinct parts of the work environment. Error seems to be directly connected to operational complexity and procedural-goal or operational-goal conflicts. These are two (of the many) error-provoking or error-likely conditions that seem to be quasi-predictable. Knowing humans make mistakes is vital. Knowing the conditions in which mistake making may increase seems predictably smart on your part.

29

The more complex the work is to perform, the more errors we know we will have because error is directly connected to operational complexity, therefore the higher the potential for this specific work to fail. So, as we place workers in more and more complex environments, we can expect to see more and more normal human fallibility. We put highly-skilled workers into highly-complex environments and we are often shocked that they make mistakes. Complexity always creates error opportunities.

Operational-goal conflicts or production-goal conflicts are the places within your organization's processes and activities that demands the worker decide between the lesser of two evils. "The rule says I should do X, but I really must do Y." These goal conflicting areas are best understood as the places in your process (you most certainly will not know where these places are in your process, but you can best believe you have many!) where we have created a conundrum, some type of operational or intellectual discomfort, for the worker to solve in order to simply bring about production.

Error is connected to the complexity of work. The more complex the work is to accomplish, the greater the potential for a mistake to happen during the performance of tasks. Think of complexity as defined as the degree to which this work is made up of many discrete steps that are tightly coupled to their completion. Complexity and complications are different; more on that later. Add to the performance of complex work the potential for processes, procedures, rules and directives to create conflicts. The more rigid the procedure is written, the greater the potential there is to require variance from the procedure. Since work is always accompanied with variability, the potential for a rule to be difficult to follow increases. Remember, plans don't typically predict unexpected events, and no procedure is ever complete enough to include all the potential unexpected events that could happen while work is being performed. This reminds us that we can't really fix errors, we make the system flexible enough to manage the error consequence.

Why people make errors is interesting. When people make errors is always based upon opportunity. How people make errors is the topic for some very interesting books and studies. The bottom line is that this first principle doesn't spend a lot of time building error-management controls or trying to control the uncontrollable. We don't really worry about the details and specifics around human error, we simply attest that the error is common, frequent, and normal and build space in our work design for recovery.

Perhaps it is better just to say, and in fact this is exactly what the original principle says in clear language, every worker, even your very best, makes mistakes. Mistakes are normal and happen all the time. Every failure you have had has included mistakes. Every success you have had also has included mistakes. Human error is normal; you won't fix it, you won't reduce it, you can't imagine all the ways it can happen.

Error Defined

I spend a lot of time talking about and defining human error with people all over the globe. When I say a lot of time, I mean a lot of time. I figure that I must spent roughly 30 minutes a day, five days a week, talking about human fallibility and error as a normal part of operations. I have been working in the field of Human Performance for almost 30 years; that would make my total professional discussion time about human error 1,885 hours (or 113,100 minutes) in the last three decades. 113,100 minutes is a lot of time, and it sounds repetitious and boring, but I think the time is well spent.

Helping people understand the normalness of human error is fundamental to shifting organizational programs away from a traditional blame and punish environment towards a more enlightened understanding of systems and reliability. We don't manage the absence or presence of error. Error is never a choice. Error can't be a choice because you do not choose to make an error or mistake. Error happens because people are fundamentally fallible.

Let's define error: Error is the unintentional deviation from an expected outcome. Human error means that something has been done that was "not intended by the actor; not desired by a set of rules or an external observer; or that led the task or system outside its acceptable limits".[5] In short, it is a deviation from intention, expectation or desirability. Logically, human actions can fail to achieve their goal in two different ways: the actions can go as planned, but the plan can be inadequate (leading to mistakes); or, the plan can be satisfactory, but the performance can be deficient (leading to mental slips, mental lapses, or operational assumptions).[6]

In short, errors and mistakes are simply errors and mistakes. These deviations are not a product of conscious actions; in fact, more often than not, these errors and mistakes are the product of an unintentional deviation. Even more interesting is that these unintentional deviations are not detectable as deviations while the deviation is occurring. The deviation in practice looks exactly like normal work until the deviation is amplified and identified by consequence.

No matter how you cut it, because human error is unintentional and unexpected, human error is **not** a choice and therefore not controlled by asking people to be more careful or attentive. We can't prevent errors by asking people not to make mistakes. In many ways, the belief that error is some type of misguided intention is even scarier in that this belief means asking for different behavior will cause

---

[5] Senders, J.W. and Moray, N.P. (1991) *Human Error: Cause, Prediction, and Reduction.* Lawrence Erlbaum Associates, p.25. ISBN 0-89859-598-3.

[6] Hollnagel, E. (1993) *Human Reliability Analysis Context and Control.* Academic Press Limited. ISBN 0-12-352658-2.

different outcomes. Asking somebody not to do something they did not mean to do in the hopes that this person will not do what they did not intend to do in the first place, again, is a gigantic waste of time. We do it all the time and it is really ill-advised.

As strange as this all must sound, the concept that human error and mistakes are normal is a hard concept to sell to your organization, hence the 113,100-minute investment on my part. The idea that error is some type of moral or operational failure is hard-wired into our thinking and therefore, error being bad is hard-wired into our investigation and cause determination process. We have entire categories of cause that are called "human error" and despite our efforts to avoid using these categories, the "human error as the reason the bad thing happened" idea drifts into our biases and in our findings and in our reporting and, most damaging, deep into our understanding of how the bad event happened. Error determination is a powerful bias that has been blocking event learning for a very long time. We tend to focus on how the worker failed our system, which leaves fragile and poorly designed systems in place, waiting for the next poor error-maker to make a mistake resulting in a similar failure.

The Not-So-Strange Relationship Between Error and Violation

So, what about "honest mistakes," you may ask? I get that question quite a bit.

I will be bold and upfront with you when I say that I don't really know what the term "honest mistake" means. If there are honest mistakes does that mean there are dishonest mistakes? I find this question usually leads to the very common management struggle between the concept of error and the concept of violation. Managers want to feel good about themselves and they want to be perceived as fair and just leaders, doing a good job leading the organization. These managers want you to know they don't punish for making honest mistakes.

However, in saying they don't punish honest mistakes these same managers are leaving the door open to punish dishonest mistakes, or as managers like to call them "violations." Violations are clean and seductive. The worker purposely chose to break a rule and that means the worker chose his or her fate. We can't have violations of our rules in our organizations; that idea is untenable. There must be a line between error and violation and managers must have the power to react to both differently. This all sounds good, but sadly that is not the way work in the workplace plays itself out. The line between error and violation is often very fuzzy. Who draws that line, and when that line is drawn, makes a huge difference in how we understand and explain the events that take place.

You could make a pretty good case that a violation is not a mistake because a violation is the product of a knowing and fully-aware choice to *fail* do something that the worker was supposed to do or do something they are *not* supposed to do. Choice is important for determining intention and intention is important for understanding error. In short, I think about error and violation like this: If the worker purposely chose to violate the rule, did this same worker assume this choice would lead to the specific consequence that happened? When we say a worker made a bad choice we are also saying at the exact same time that this worker *purposely did not* select all the right choices that could have been selected. What I find is that workers react operationally based upon production and efficiency; almost never are worker reactions examined for possible consequences. If you drop a knife in your kitchen you have a couple choices: You can try to grab the falling knife (awful choice) or you can jump back and save your feet (better choice). The question becomes did you have time to think about the rightness and wrongness of this decision, or is this more of a reaction in the moment to the hazard of a falling knife?

This discussion gets a bit emotional, so hang on while you are having it with your organization.

The differences (and simularities) between error and violation has led some large organizations to amend these principles to

The Principles

Organizations influence their systems and people. The application of Human Performance principles makes it easier for people to be successful.

1. People make mistakes.
2. People's actions are rarely malicious, but well-meaning behaviors intended to get the job done.
3. Unexpected events may be a symptom of a weakness in our systems.
4. We can detect, manage and prevent most error-likely situations.
5. Understanding the context surrounding error, and implementing defenses based upon learning can help reduce the severity of incidents.
6. Organizations and leaders influence individual behavior.
7. How leaders respond to failure matters; suspend judgment and respond with curiosity.

How error-tolerant are our systems?

include an additional principle; worker violation is almost always a function of the worker not following the process because it makes sense at the time to not follow that process. One major international global benchmarking organization has added a principle that says, "Violations are rarely, if ever, malicious, but are well meaning behaviors intended to get the job done." [7] I like this added principle because early on it establishes a deeper understanding of error. I also think it is smart in that this additional principle helps to set the idea of worker violations aside as if they are special and unique (they don't seem to be either special or unique in actual organizations, but it allows managers to think less emotionally and more theoretically) in order to "create dialogue and fluency" around the similarities that exist between error and violation. What is a violation if it is not an error? The answer is that it depends on context; how we choose to see the event and to a great extent the consequence of the event.

I am not naïve (ok, I am probably super naïve). I know there are and will be violations of rules, processes, and policies. I know that people violate rules for selfish reasons and personal gain, but I would submit that these types of actual violations are exceptionally rare. My problem is that in the vast majority of events that I have been allowed to analyze and learn from, I have rarely seen flagrant violation of policy for personal gain. That is not to say it does not exist, because it does. I am certain and convinced that most of the violations we see involve normal workers trying to do normal work (they aren't stealing, drinking, or saboteur-ing the organization); they are just normal workers who intentionally varied work practices for a good

---

[7] This slide is taken loosely from a Global Benchmarking Meeting document held by Oil and Gas in order to share best practices around Human Performance in 2017. Many major companies have adopted these principles for HPI/HOP. You can see the influence of INPO, DOE, and evidence of the administrative struggle between the definition of error and violation.

reason in order to get work done efficiently. I am also hesitant to set our standard on the extreme case example, like a saboteur working in your organization. If you set your policies around extreme cases you get extreme interpretations of your policies. If you hire a lot of saboteurs you don't have a Human Performance problem, you have a giant Human Resources problem; those are very different issues to be sure.

Error is Not All Bad:
The Difference Between Good or Lucky

Not all error is bad. Error without consequence tells us where our systems are robust and functioning and where errors and mistakes are possible. I know it sounds odd to say that an error that is discovered without significant consequence is a good way for the organization to learn, but in fact, I think error identification is a very effective, predictive data point. Close Call, Near Miss, or Near Hit reporting has tried to capture this type of information for a long time. We, as an industry have been quite effective in seeing Near Hit reporting as valuable and generally we are quite good at celebrating identified close calls as opportunities for deliberate improvement. We tend to ask why a near miss failed to have consequence; this is great information and can allow our organizations to learn a great deal. However, I am not certain that simply learning why the bad thing didn't happen is enough for organizations to learn all there is to learn. We tend to become fixated on what could have happened as opposed to really looking at how the process and system allowed the failure to occur; that is really an important way to look at managing close call reporting information. I think we tend to look at these near misses as what could have happened as opposed to looking at what actually happened.

This challenge is fabulously illuminated by two simple words, two simple ideas: "good and lucky." Whether your organization was good or lucky is the difference between your organization's capacity to fail safely, let's call this capacity "error tolerance," and your organization's ability to catch a lucky break, averting a terrible accident. Both good and lucky are reasonable and potential outcomes, yet the data these near events contain changes quite a bit when you ask different questions.

There are two types of near events, near misses, near hits or close calls.[8] The first type is when a bad thing occurs and it is simply luck that separates your organization's workers from some type of bad outcome. This type of near miss is the "lucky" type of event. The only thing that kept the accident from happening is "chance or luck." Your organization got lucky. The second type of event is when a bad thing occurs and your organization has an accident, but consequences were minimal because a safeguard or safeguards were triggered and the safeguard worked. The safeguard functioned exactly the way the control was designed to function. The accident is a near miss because

[8] In this book, I am attempting to use every possible name I can think of to talk about an event that almost happened, was recognized as potentially significant, and was hopefully celebrated by the organization that had the event. Organizations are really emotionally tied to what these are called. I am trying to accommodate everyone.

your safety system had predicted the potential for this failure to occur and your organization had somehow put barriers in place to reduce the potential impact of the event. In reality, a "good near miss" is the most aggressive and effective test your organization could ever undertake to prove that your safety systems are robust, effective, and valuable.

When faced with a near miss report, or in the creation of a near miss reporting culture, perhaps it is better to ask if the organization was "good" or if the organization was "lucky?" This allows a better understanding of the event and a better identification of the error condition that surrounded the event in question. Changing the question from who failed to a much more valuable question of what worked and were we "good or lucky" changes the entire tenor of the conversation. Your organization is not really interested in the error that was made, in fact your organization becomes much more interested in the ability of your process and systems to contain the failure – to fail safely – and understand and actually test the resilience capacity within your organization in real time. Do you see how the response to the error is more important than the actual error itself?

Suddenly the error becomes the trigger and not the cause. The error triggered your safety and reliability safeguards into action. That is quite a turn in thinking from a more traditional organization; this way of thinking is pretty far from the "old school" method of determining who made a mistake and asking for a promise to not err again. The cause doesn't live within the error. The error is no longer very interesting. The cause lives inside the conditions present or absent within your ability to do this work in a safe and stable manner. The cause becomes interlinked with recovery and control. Were the right safeguards in place when we needed them? The error actually made it possible to understand the efficacy of your controls, not the potential for a worker to make an error of some type; you already know workers are good at making mistakes. You can manage controls; controls are real and knowable. You can't manage errors because errors seem to move beyond prediction. You don't know who or why or even when a worker will make a mistake, but it may be your best worker or your worst worker (they both exist in your organization); error doesn't seem to delineate between the two.

With this new twist in the way your organization views worker error, an entirely new way of thinking about failure has been unlocked and a completely different way to gather information and learning has been created, becoming a powerful tool for your organization to use. What is important is that this new way of thinking is occurring because error is normal and people make mistakes, not in spite of fallible workers working to be perfect. The potential changes for your workers (workers are truly experts on your system) to become engaged not as the origin of failure (the mistake makers), but as the experts on system recovery and error tolerance (the brilliant insiders who know where you are strong and where you are weak on controls). Engaging workers as problem identifiers and not as problem makers changes everything.

Workers are not the problem, workers are the problem identifiers; this new view of safety starts to become apparent at all levels of your

41

management process. The first principle of Human Performance only really makes sense if your organization is willing to change the way your organization sees its workers. You will really appreciate this change and you will deliberately get better.

Good Systems are Tolerant Systems

I have some important news for you, the first principle of human performance is not really about error. I think I have made a case that error is neither unusual or intentional. Error is so normal that error is not very interesting or ever the cause of a failure. Human error is about tolerance and recoverability. Can we fail at a point in the process and recover in such a way that we avoid significant operational upset? That question simply stipulates that errors will be made; we don't know when, don't know who, maybe not even know how, but the error will be made. When that error occurs are we robust enough to recover effectively and gracefully? Do we have one more trip around the earth before we land?[9]

Human error becomes the trigger to examine your systems. Identification of failure becomes important because it tells the story of system response. The story of system response is a much more profitable and effective way to determine your organizational

---

[9] This idea comes from a conversation with David Woods. A group of us were hanging out and chatting about what Professor Woods calls "graceful extensibility" where he decides to tell the story of landing a spacecraft back on earth. "If the mission is not ready," Dr. Woods said, "they always have one more orbit around the earth to get ready." Try as I might, I can't get that story out of my mind. It pops up all the time.

capacity to create stability, safety and production for a sustainable operational future.

The Problem with Being Wrong

How do I know when an error is an error? When does an error become an error? Is there a line a worker crosses between not making an error and making an error? How close can I get to that line and still be safe? Is an error without a negative outcome an error? One of the biggest challenges with the realization that human error is normal is how difficult it is to identify error before there is consequence. Remember, errors become very explicit and easy to identify after these errors have consequence. This is why in retrospect error is often seen as a choice, but in context error is much more difficult to identify and much more of a reaction to current operational activities.

The biggest challenge with human error is before you know you have made an error it feels exactly like you are doing the work correctly; before you

> **The Problem with being wrong is that before you know you are wrong it feels exactly like being right.**

know you're wrong it feels exactly like you're right. The perceived difference is difficult to discern. It is generally true (and something that I try to remember when I look at failure) that it is very difficult for a worker or workers to identify something that has not yet

43

happened. Before consequence arises, it is remarkably hard to imagine such an outcome. Add to this equation the important point that the likelihood of the process you are working on failing is at best, uncertain, and naturally unimaginable. We execute our work thinking we will be successful in completing our work. People are fallible, but they are also optimistic. We fail and yet we believe we will succeed. The crazy part of all of this is that we mostly *do* succeed. Workers are mostly successful because they can quickly detect and correct errors while performing work. Even when we fail, we end up succeeding most of the time.

People Make Mistakes

The most important discussion about the first principle of Human Performance is error is so normal the error itself is often not interesting. I promise you will get to the point that when you are learning from and understanding events in your organization, the actual error made by a worker or operator will not be very important to your event review and corrective action process. Error, once you understand how normal it is, becomes pretty obvious in the event review. You will become much more interested in the fact that you are conducting work in an environment that is not tolerant of inevitable error. Suddenly, the absence or presence of error is not the problem; error is a fact. The problem will become the identification of a system with a lack of tolerance for failure. That is an incredibly important finding. I used to worry about error. I don't worry so much about error anymore; error is just normal. Now what I worry about are working conditions that thwart are not error tolerant, systems that

44

are so brittle that when the predictable error occurs, the error results in unacceptable consequence for the organization. There is not enough time for one more trip around the earth. That operational context, brittle and fragile, is scary to me.

I know that "error is normal" or "error is not interesting" are not very helpful statements if you are early in Human Performance thinking within your organization. Early on in the journey, I know error is interesting and attractive. Errors are seductive because they look manageable, so we should be managing them. If we could just identify all the places workers will screw up and fix those places we would be so far ahead of this problem. This idea is attractive.

I can remember early on in the human performance journey of my organization attending a meeting with other like-minded Human Performance coordinators. This was during the early days of the Human Performance program for the Department of Energy. Cindy Wagner, Shane Bush, Bill Rigot, and I were in a meeting where we collectively and quite excitedly decided that if we could predict every place an error would happen and remove the error-likely conditions (which would then remove the error from the work) we would create the safest organizations in the world.[10] It is normal to be attracted to error management because error management seems so linear and predictable. The problem with error management is that error itself is

---

[10] This was at an EFCOG Meeting, the US Department of Energy Contractors Forum. Cindy Wagner was the incoming Chair of the HPI Sub-committee, Shane Bush was the outgoing Chair. I was trying to shed as much responsibility as possible. This meeting was in the Albuquerque Training Center and was held around 2005. Donuts were served.

not linear, *not* predictable, and incredibly normal. We maintained that line of thinking for a couple of years. I think from a developmental and program maturity approach, starting with a robust error discussion is extremely important. You can't really improve as an organization if you don't build a collective understanding that people make mistakes.

There will come a time when human error will not be very interesting to you. Error will become less and less a part of how you see events, how you see threats to stability, and ultimately how you see risk. Error is normal, so therefore, controls and recovery become vital.

I promise, the more you think about this first principle: People Make Mistakes, the less interesting human error becomes. Error is normal and by definition if error is normal it is not very interesting. Error is so normal is it never causal, which makes errors less interesting. Most importantly, errors and mistakes happen both when systems succeed and when systems fail; it is less important whether the outcome is a success, failure, or both. That is why "People Make Mistakes" is such a great first principle. Error is real and normal and we should not design work systems that count on workers not making errors and mistakes, that count on workers being perfect.

That said, the people in your organization are going to need to discuss this, from the beginning, and over and over again. You will probably never stop talking to your organization about how human error is not the target of your investigation and learning processes. Human error is where you begin to identify why your organizational systems were so brittle that when an error was made when work was being conducted, the system was not prepared or ready for the outcome. You will have this conversation many, many times and each time is important. People do make mistakes.

Chapter Three

Principle Number Two

Blame Fixes Nothing

- Blame is emotionally important, not operationally important
- Blame makes error a choice in retrospect
- Blame takes up emotional and intellectual space with little added value
- Blame misdirects resources and strategies
- Blame is the opposite of encouragement
- Deterrence by Blaming is not effective

People achieve high levels of performance because of the encouragement and reinforcement received from leaders, peers, and subordinates.

The organization is perfectly tuned to get the performance it receives from the workforce. All human behavior, good and bad, is reinforced, whether by immediate consequences or by past experience. A behavior is reinforced by the consequences that an individual experience when the behavior occurs. The level of safety and reliability of a facility is directly dependent on the behavior of people. Further, human performance is a function of behavior. Because behavior is influenced by the consequence's workers experience, what happens to workers when they exhibit certain behaviors is an important factor in improving human performance. Positive and immediate reinforcement for expected behaviors is ideal.[11]

---

[11] Excerpt taken from the DOE Standard, Human Performance Improvement Handbook, Volume 1. Concepts and Standards, DOE-HDBK-1028-2009 June 2009.

One Problem: We think bad things happen to bad people

"We think bad things happen to bad people." When I say that phrase out loud in a workshop often people become angry and offended. This statement almost always elicits an emotional response from organizational leaders. That emotional response from both workers and leaders is the very reason why I say bad things happen to bad people. I want folks to respond emotionally. I want them to think about this as an important part of their organization's culture that must be changed. The idea we believe bad things happen to bad people is an offensive idea to most people. Those same people respond by telling me "bad things happen to *bad* people" is simply not true, or at least they don't think that way. In fact, most people believe they are enlightened enough to think beyond that shallow and offensive idea. I would guess the people who get especially upset with this idea must think that bad things happen to all people. We like to think bad things don't happen to bad people. We want to think the best about people. I want you to think the best about people and about me. The problem is, we tend to judge a worker in retrospect and find the place or places where there is a bad decision, a bad action, or a bad assumption that must have caused the event in question. Our systems and often our thinking absolutely reflect the idea that because a bad outcome has happened, somebody must have done something wrong. Somebody messed up badly.

The judgement of weak moral or intellectual character after an event is:

1. A perfectly normal response for better or worse. A response, I must add, that has been around a long, long time in the history of humankind. We have an urgent need to find a reason why something bad just occurred and the most available target for that reason is normally human frailty and faults.

2. Not quite as cut and dry as saying bad things happen to bad people. We are bit more nuanced in the way we call people bad. We often say the worker failed to follow the procedures, which is a nice way to say a better worker would have followed the rules. If I had a dollar for every time someone said these words: "you can't fix stupid!" I would be driving an extravagant car. A smarter worker, a more experienced worker, a more alert worker, or a worker that cares more would have ensured a much better outcome.

I will admit I may be overstating this case for effect. We hardly ever say "bad things happen to bad people" in real life. We have, however, created enormous lists of ways to blame workers without actually saying they are bad people doing bad things. We still say it, but we have created an entire language to allow our organizations to pass judgement after the fact on a worker or workers that doesn't sound like we are actually passing judgement. I would invite you to look at your organization's investigation reporting and findings documents and read them through the "bad things happen to bad people filter" and see if you see hints of this way of thinking. We have many socially acceptable ways to say the event that occurred or nearly occurred, happened because a person (worker, supervisor, contractor) was the weakest link in the system and that weak link failed the systems. The person was, at the crucial moment, deficient in some way. What scares me is how easy it is to determine the worker is insufficient in his or her actions and opinions after failure occurs. It is really obvious somebody messed up; that is why we are here meeting about this failure.

In traditional safety practice, we see worker errors and mistakes as a problem to be fixed. When an accident happens, we actively seek through quite formal investigations the exact place where the worker made a bad decision, a wrong choice, an at-risk behavior, or a mistake and we deem that the

> **Don't Limit Yourself to the Quest for Worker Error or Procedural Non-Compliance…**
>
> **You Will Always Find Both.**

place where the worker weakness failed the system as the problem. We then stop our analysis, halt the investigation, and then begin to create some elaborate and often expensive way to fix the worker so that this same undesirable behavior does not happen again. We have found the problem and the person who created the problem. Now we can fix the problem by fixing the person who failed the organization. This process is often called, quite accurately: Name, Blame, Shame, and Retrain.

Sometimes we try to fix the offending worker just to send a message to the rest of the workers that we are aware that any worker could fail and they should be watching as an example is being made of the bad worker. We often send the entire workforce to training to tell them not to do what the offending worker did. This represents the old "one guy sneezes and everybody gets a Kleenex" theory for corrective actions. Many organizations make the worker speak publicly at a safety meeting about how bad they were in causing an accident. We drive the offending worker to the "edge of the village" to think about how they failed the company. Worse still, sometimes we fire the worker for misbehaving in order to support a set of cardinal rules that must be followed by all workers all of the time. All of these corrective actions seem like actions, but really do nothing except formally place blame. Corrective actions must address much more than blame.

We really do think bad things happen to bad people. Bad accidents happen to workers who are not as good as good workers. A better worker would have done the job right and not gotten hurt. At almost every investigation I have ever conducted, somebody will lean back and say, "If I were doing that job I would have stopped the work activity right here, before the failure and harm was caused". That comment is impressive at so many levels. First the idea the person who made that comment could actually do the work is usually unrealistic, secondly knowing how the event ends influences everything that is said, written, and even thought about in the investigation, and thirdly thinking that the worker could have even imagined the unwanted outcome is unrealistic and unfair.

As much as we don't want to believe it, we have created a world that responds to bad events by deeming some poor worker a bad person, or maybe it is better to say the poor worker had a momentary lack of judgement while performing work. Thinking this way saves time and protects the organization's systems, processes, and honor, however the idea that a better worker would have made a better choice is simply not true and most importantly did not occur.

Determining What Happened by Talking About What Did Not Happen

Want to know the quickest way to get to blame? Investigate what should have happened. This might be the time to talk about blame and blame's amazing ability to take an entire organization and force this same organization into counter-factual thinking. In my opinion, nothing is more offensive, more inaccurate, or more blaming then defining an event by discussing what should have happened. Every moment an organization spends discussing what should have happened, or what failed to happen in order to investigate an event is a complete waste of time. We want to look at what did happen. We want to understand what conditions had to exist in order to provoke the failure that occurred. We can only understand the event by discussing what actually happened. Knowing and talking about what did not happen is not helpful because those things did not happen.

Counter factual analysis always leads to the identification of a deficiency. Counter factual thinking can only lead to a discussion of what did not happen, which then leads the organization to an even longer discussion about why the things that should have happened did not happen, which leads the team to an eventual determination of blame. Blame leads to some type of punishment, either actual or perceived punishment (and perceived punishment is actual punishment). Two days without pay is punishment. Mandatory "eyes on path" training for everyone in the organization is also perceived by the receivers of the training as punishment. Counter factual thinking always leads to blame. Blame does not fix the system.

Counter factual assessments are not wrong; counter factual assessments are the beginning of the explanation and not the end product of an investigation. When you are trying to understand what happened in an event, you start with what didn't happen and that discussion should lead you to an accurate description of what actual happened. Don't stop your investigation with only counter factual assessments because counter factual assessments give your organization an investigation of what your organization wished would have happened and not a description of what actually happened. It is also much more important to move the organizational response towards learning and improvement and away from blame. Worst case is ending an inquiry with blame because blame fixes nothing.

Blame Makes Mistakes Choices – Mistakes are Never Choices.

Mistakes are not choices and errors are not a conscious decision to fail. Error is an unintentional deviation from an expected outcome.

54

Mistakes are not intentional failings and, most importantly, deep down we know that. The problem is we simply can't stop thinking about this the way we have historically considered this. There must be some way that a better person would have known to make a better assessment of risk and make better operational decisions.

Yet, we still judge error as some type of deliberate action. We really do. We have a strong need to make judgement about perceived bad actions and decisions that lead to some type of operational or personal cost. We want to distance ourselves from the action or decision by saying that "had we been in that position, we would have made a different decision," and we want to separate ourselves from the offending worker. In a way, we want to say this person is different from other people because they made an error. The crazy thing is that when we think that way we almost always end up fixing nothing.

An Awful Case Study

A couple of years ago, a school bus in Chattanooga, Tennessee crashed. Here is the news article on the response by the State of Tennessee to this event:

> A bus driver on trial for his role in the death of six elementary school students was found guilty Thursday on numerous charges stemming from a crash in November 2016.
>
> The Driver was transporting 37 students from Woodmore Elementary School in Chattanooga, Tennessee, when the bus he was driving flipped over and crashed into a tree, killing six children between the ages of 6 and 10.
>
> The Driver originally faced 34 charges, according to online court records, including six counts of vehicular homicide, but was found guilty on six lesser charges of criminal negligent homicide.
>
> He also faced a variety of assault charges, in addition to one charge of reckless endangerment, one charge of reckless driving and one charge of the use of a portable electronic device by a school bus driver. [12]

I won't argue about the court's right to punish the guilty and I won't argue the need to make a bad person accountable (really the word we should use is culpable) for the needless and painful death of 6 children. I, also, feel a great need to punish the guilty. Bad people

---

[12] Taken from CNN, "Chattanooga School Bus Driver Found Guilty of 6 Students Deaths in Crash," March 2, 2016.

should not get away with doing bad things. Justice must be served. Little children should never die in an accident.

I will argue that in our need to punish the guilty (a bad person did a bad thing), we satisfy our emotional, almost primal urge to punish and yet what does jailing this driver fix? Did busses across the nation become safer? Did airbags or seatbelts or roll cages get placed in busses across the country? Can you assure me this event will not happen again to another bus with another driver in another place? Honestly, what did we learn? Perhaps more importantly, from a corrective action effectiveness standpoint, what did we fix? The belief that a better driver would have had a better outcome may be true, but it is incredibly over-simplified.

This bus crash makes me feel angry and powerless because there are many of us in the world who know better and would challenge this culpability thinking publicly. It makes me feel angry that 6 small children died doing something as normal as going to school on a public-school bus. What makes me most angry and unsettled is that we met pain with pain.[13] We may have gotten some definition of justice in that we punished the guilty person, the bad actor, but did we learn anything? Did we get better and did we deliberately

---

[13] The idea of never meeting pain with pain and the idea of restorative responses to workplace accidents is a special area of interest for Sidney Dekker. I am constantly amazed at how Professor Dekker has become a strong voice for learning and improvement by using restorative concepts to move operations forward. I must say this idea has influenced my work, my life, and my thinking more than any other. Thanks Sidney. Stay true. Steel on steel.

improve? Blaming, although sometimes emotionally satisfying, fixes nothing.

What I find frightening in our organizational learning and investigation products are example after example of emotional reactions to events. Those emotional reactions are seen in punishment, retraining, and awareness, challenges, and admissions of guilt by all parties involved. These types of reactions are counterproductive. They give the organization the "feeling" that the organization has done something, when in fact, the organization has fixed nothing. That is the problem with blame, blame fixes nothing, but satisfies our desire to find blame. Finding blame does not lead to improvement.

Error is Not a Choice

When we think bad things happen to bad people, we automatically think error is a choice that was poorly made by a worker who should have known better. We can't imagine how unlikely the terrible outcome would have seemed to the worker at the time, since this worker was a part of the conditions that created such an event that had yet to fail. We expect some type of organizational justice that suggests the worker must have known the consequences of the choice he or she was making before the choice led to a bad outcome. That is a clean argument in retrospect. You will always know the outcome after the event has occurred, the problem is that starting an investigation with this information does not accurately assess what went on prior to the event taking place.

We don't know the future and people are bad at forecasting the future.

We assume, or retrospective bias leads us to assume, that somehow the outcome was knowable, understandable, and accessible to the worker who was about to face a surprise upset condition he or she did not know would occur. Sadly, that is not how life works; we almost never get to write an ending prospectively. I promise that if I knew I was going to get hurt I would not have done what I did to get injured. We are so much smarter in retrospect. I am 100% accurate at predicting winning lottery numbers after the lottery drawing has already occurred. I am so incredibly smart after the event has occurred.

Blame Makes Error a Choice in Retrospect

We really want to believe that workers are making choices to be safe while they are working. The problem is the idea that somehow, we choose to do good and/or bad things is entirely dependent on knowing what is good and bad in the actual context of work.

It is hard not to judge error as some type of worker deficiency. I know, from my own experience, that we are quick to determine the quality of a person (especially if that person is us, we are our own harshest critics), after an error occurs. Criticism, after the fact, is commonplace as evidenced by observing the way workers and managers beat themselves up after an event occurs. One of the most difficult aspects of event recovery is to help remove self-blame. We are almost always our own harshest critics, and this criticism is a part of the struggle we develop in trying to understand human error. Knowing that we did something wrong seems to close some mysterious cosmic uncertainty in the universe. All of us, if we have managed people before, know that when an event occurs, the "offending worker" often will come into our office and "fall on his or her sword." When a worker tells you that they messed up (self-blame), it is your job to say to them, "I know it must feel that way, but if we stop learning when we recognize you made a mistake, all we will learn is that you are a normal human being." We assume, organizationally, the mistake is the problem; get better people, people who make less mistakes, and our system is stable and dependable once again. In fact, the mistake is the trigger that exposes deeper flaws and absent controls in our processes and systems.

Blame is powerful in quickly making the determination of who is at fault. Blame causes culpability to be placed on the bad worker. Blame is very seductive because it is so simple and so clean. Finding blame is way easier then fixing processes. Finding blame holds a person accountable for the failure after the failure occurs and also removes accountability for the failure of the larger system, process, or organization. The problem is finding blame fixes nothing.

Our Accounting Systems Make Us Do It

I am convinced our collective move towards blame and punishment within our organizations has slowly drifted towards negativity with positive intentions. I think the tendency to look at the workers first is our event accounting systems has forced us to select cause from a predetermined list that was created to collect data and not to explain failure, learn, and improve. The need to track and trend failure data has been a dominant force in the way we determine the difference between organizations that are considered safety and organizations that are considered unsafety. We have entire categories of causal factors that are called "human error" and try as we might to avoid using these categories, the "human error" as the reason a bad thing transpired drifts into our bias, findings and reporting and, most damaging, deep into our understanding of how a bad event occurred. Error determination establishes a powerful bias that has been blocking us from learning from events for a very long time. We become fixated on how the worker failed our system, which leaves fragile and poorly designed systems intact, awaiting the next poor error-maker to make a mistake.

The case for why this has not helped our programs mature past this idea has been made many times before. We know that tracking similar events feels like learning, and yet is not very meaningful for our programs operationally. The idea is that if we could show trends of how events are occurring in our organizations, we could go out and focus our efforts on those specific areas and see improvement from our efforts to fix our problems. In theory, that should work if our events are linear and predictable. In practice, our events seem to be more non-linear and much more like "outliers" then repeat occurrences. We have systemized blame in our tracking and accounting processes; the challenge will be removing this institutionalized blame from our organizations.

Blaming Fixes Nothing

Every minute you spend blaming a worker for an event is a minute of your life you will not get back. Blaming a person for an event is like getting to the airport 4 hours early, it works because you make your plane, but you lose so much of your soul and so much of your life in the meantime. Blame does not provide sustainable improvement and fixes nothing.

Even more importantly, the need to blame someone for the event does not change the outcome of the event. Perhaps the most profound realization is knowing that the outcome doesn't really care about the cause. If a worker gets killed, the family of the worker does not feel better if we determine the worker made a bad decision, at-risk behavior, or a mistake; the worker is dead and blaming the worker for being dead helps no one. Our challenge is to avoid focusing on finding blame for the event that just occurred. Our job is to understand and explain the event so that we can look forward at the other conditions and similar circumstances that exist in our organization and place controls and safeguards to thwart the next event in a sustainable way. We don't arrive at the latter solution when we stop with the first solution. Don't find blame, fix systems.

Chapter Four

Principle Number Three

Learning and Improving is Vital

- Organizations have two choices when responding to failure: to learn and improve or to blame and punish; learning is a strategic and operational choice toward improvement.
- Learning is a deliberate improvement strategy.
- Knowing how work is done is difficult.
- Workers are the experts, the profound users of the work process.
- Workers always complete the process design.
- Defenses are placed in systems, tested in systems, and strengthened in systems by learning how successful work is done.

Events can be avoided through an understanding of the reason or reasons mistakes occur and application of the lessons learned from past events (or errors).

Traditionally, improvement in human performance has resulted from corrective actions derived from an analysis of facility events and issue reports, a method that reacts to what happened in the past.

Learning from our mistakes and the mistakes of others is reactive, after the fact, but important for continuous improvement. Human performance improvement today requires a combination of both proactive and reactive approaches. Anticipating how an event or error can be prevented is proactive and is a more cost-effective means of preventing events and issues from developing.[14]

Learning and Improving is Vital

You have heard it said a billion times, "you don't know what you don't know." It is true of course; you can't know what you don't know and there is much you don't know. There is hope, however, and that hope is in your organization's ability to continually learn. Learning is vital to continued successful operations. In short, learning may be the most powerful safety and reliability tool you have.

It has become trendy to say you want your organization to be a "learning organization." You do want to become that type of organization, but simply saying you are a learning organization is far from actually becoming one. Learning takes effort, deliberate resourcing, and courage. Your organization has to be humble enough to know what you don't know. Your organization has to be smart enough to know that you can benefit by greater knowledge. Remember this, knowing less does not make you smarter. Only knowing more makes your organization better.

---

[14] Excerpt taken from the DOE Standard, Human Performance Improvement Handbook, Volume 1. Concepts and Standards, DOE-HDBK-1028-2009 June 2009.

When we talk about learning, we are really talking about the way your organization answers these three questions:

1. What systems, processes, and tools do you have to openly elicit feedback from your organization, about your organization? How easy to use and available are these tools to every level of your workforce?
2. How open is your organization to actually receiving honest feedback about your operations? How comfortable are you with hearing bad news? Do you embrace the "red areas" and question the "green areas" of your organization? How often do you punish the feedback messengers by, for example, assigning them more work?
3. How committed is your organization to make changes based upon the information you get from your workers? If you ask for feedback (both good and bad) you must also do something with the feedback that you gather; trust is built by making agreements with your workers and then, most importantly, keeping those agreements in a timely manner.

In your organization, there are many things you don't know and cannot know. By the very nature of your position, whatever your position is, you are separated from the work-as-actually-done. Managers see work differently from workers and senior leaders see work differently from other managers. Everybody has a very distinct and different understanding of how work is actually done. No matter where you are in the organization, you won't know how work is done around your organization by workers who actually conduct work.

You will never fully know the struggles your workers encounter while conducting work that exists in your organization because you will rarely, if ever, do the work that your workers do. You don't fully realize the difficulties workers encounter using your systems and processes while actually conducting work. Workers, leaders, and managers are constantly solving problems and adapting systems to try and ensure production success. Workers work and leaders lead and those functions are very different. This fact will never change. In a way, we are somewhat trapped in the context within which we work. The higher up you are in the organization, the farther away you are from the actual workplace hazards on the production floor. The lower you are in the organization, the farther away you are from having influence over the systems and processes that are used to control the work environment. We have somehow decoupled actual risk from the actual process and we are often surprised by the problems this misalignment can create.

Perhaps more importantly, you can't know what your workers know because of the job you have and the role you play in your organization's structure. Looking back to your Human Performance training, we discussed the sharp and blunt ends of the organization. Workers are closest to the sharp end and regulators and shareholders are closest to the blunt end. The idea is that the highest injury potential moves towards the sharp end while the most influence over the system moves towards the blunt end, away from the actual hazards. The separation of process from risk is an important challenge in operational learning.

Workers are always on the sharp end of your organization. Workers have closer access to how work is done and closer access to the things that can hurt or kill them. The separation between those who work and those who manage has existed a long time. This separation is not new or novel. I am not sure this separation is even a problem that we could or should fix; this idea has

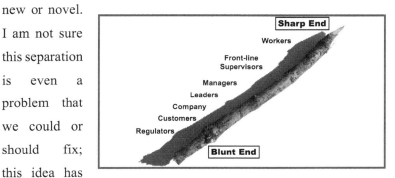

long existed in the way we conceptualize the management of work. You will always have different reasons to view work differently. It is a much different lens by which you view production and operations because of the role you play in the organization, your place on the sharp/blunt end continuum.

Knowing and guiding when and how to learn is the part of operational excellence you provide the organization. You must know when it is important to gather data and create improvement strategies. Waiting for problems to occur in order to trigger learning is old fashioned. We have done that for years and we have called them investigations. If you wait for a failure to occur, in my opinion, you are too late and too reactive. If you learn while operations are normal, going out and asking workers where the margins between safety and failure are the slimmest, you have the opportunity to respond to potential failure

67

conditions before you actually have failure. That is how learning creates improvement. Learning is a (continuous) cycle that never ends, nor should it ever end.

Learning and improving. Learning is improving. Learning is a deliberate improvement strategy – learning and improving are everything.

I want you to become comfortable with the idea of using the words learning and improving together; people who study semantics call this idea of using two words together consistently and purposefully "co-usage." These words are both individually important, but the co-usage of these two words become the secret weapon for operational excellence. Learning is the analysis and improvement is the action. Learning is the strategy and improvement is the tactic. There is a huge advantage in using the power of learning and improving as a deliberate management strategy. Your leadership team must learn and improve *deliberately*. Learning is a corrective action and has significant value. Don't let the pressure to fix something supersede the vital need to learn.

Learning is a Deliberate Improvement Strategy

Organizations don't learn by accident. Most organizations are not very good at accidental discovery; we tend to overlook information that is important in the actual "heat" of doing work. Good organizations learn deliberately. Forward-looking organizations see learning as an active improvement strategy, a sustainable and deliberate way to improve operations and processes. Thinking of operational learning as a deliberate improvement strategy allows your organization to make learning a resourced and legitimate work function. We render learning important by resourcing learning. We can measure learning and we can assess learning. We benefit through the process of learning and we improve. None of that happens without making learning a strategic improvement strategy. Build in time and resources to learn and analyze your operations on a consistent basis.

In order to create learning opportunities, your organization must first be willing to redefine what operational reliability is. Our challenge is that we have traditionally seen and measured success by tracking the absence of negative occurrences like accidents and injuries. This "reliability as an outcome to be managed" view of the world actually has reduced our organizations ability to learn and improve. We attempt to manage bad outcomes, so when something bad occurs, we often spend a huge amount of resources and effort in learning/determining how the organization failed to prevent the bad thing from occurring. Believe it or not, that is not really learning, it is trying to confirm biases that we already have.

The enemy of learning is knowing. If you think you know the answer you will not ask important, relevant questions.

When we see reliability as an operational capacity, like the gas tank in your car or the battery bar status on your mobile phone, we tend to manage the extent of safety and reliability we have, based upon activities being conducted. If you have only one bar on your phone's battery, it may not be the best way to call-in to your Monday conference call with your boss. You will most likely be forced to find another phone with a better battery charge to use for that call.

Managing reliability and safety as a capacity is a very different way to look at your organization's ability to perform stable and safe work. Because this difference is quite a change from the traditional view of safety and reliability as an outcome, your organization must learn different details. Where previously you would ask, "Who failed?" (safety as an outcome to be managed) you now start to ask "What failed?" (safety as a capacity to be monitored).

What you seek is what you will find. Knowing this bias and redefining success changes what you seek. Instead of actively deconstructing a failure after it occurs, your organization becomes much more interested in understanding how successful work is done. Understanding successful work allows you to monitor and determine the amount of capacity you have to manage operational risk for successful work. Suddenly, the lines of inquiry become focused at looking forward regarding your operations as opposed to looking backwards at your failures.

Think of learning as a corrective action. Learning is a deliberate improvement strategy, therefore going out and learning is a corrective action. Knowing more about your organization, and most importantly learning about your organization from the people who make up your organization and do your important work is never a bad thing.

Learning can be a messy and even scary process; however, the benefits far outweigh the hassle experienced for improved, more sustainable improvement. You fix the most important things first, even if you don't know what the most important things are until you start the learning process. Believing you know the answers before you ask the questions is a bad approach; it's an easy mistake to make as well. Be curious, be smart, be humble!

Think of Progress as a Vector – Metrics in Motion

Make your performance metric actual improvement in the work your organization does. Do so not by measuring individual events, but by measuring the organization's progress towards improvement. Are you improving or not? Is there greater capacity in your organization's work practices? Is the perceived knowledge of your systems so great that you no longer have any excess capacity to capture and mange failure consequences? Is your organization remaining dormant; has operational progress stalled? If so, are you trying to learn where to implement your most effective controls and processes in order to nudge your organization towards improvement again?

No fixed metric will ever be able to give you the type of information you need to learn and improve. A fixed metric will give you an assessment via a snapshot in time, but that is about all you will get. A vectoring metric gives you a better understand of the direction in which your organization is moving. That knowledge allows you to resource and monitor learning from your processes, practices, and production.

You have heard this before, but the value of getting proficient at operational learning and improving is worth repeating; our biggest challenge as people who care about safe and reliable systems is not in the *output* part of operational execution since we are good at fixing problems. The greatest challenge, and therefore the utmost improvement potential is almost always achieved by improving the learning *inputs* from your operations.

Improvement is a data **input** problem, not a data **output** problem.

If you have more comprehensive information you can craft better solutions. We tend to give less credence to the learning and analysis portion of understanding our operations in order to create and leverage more time for short-term gratification actions that fix problems. As a professional discipline, safety professionals are good at fixing problems. The larger challenge has historically been in the analysis of the more problematic aspects of our work. We have not been as good at identifying problems in our organizations. We are not experts in learning from the organization itself, nor at accessing the profound knowledge of workers.

Workers are the Experts –

Workers Always Complete Your Design

Nobody, and I really mean nobody, understands the work your organization does better than the people who actually perform the work. It seems crazy to me that we must remind each other to talk to our workers. These people work for you. You pay them. This represents information that is always available to address operational issues, identify potential problems, and to monitor and asses your organization's capacity to manage operational upsets and negative consequences.

What I find most interesting, is the idea that all of your systems and processes, rules and procedures rely on one very important factor that is completely out of your control. That should scare you at some level. You write the best document in the world and you still must count on the worker to follow the document. Even scarier, the best document in the world is not be adequate in itself to actually perform work. Procedures demand worker adaptation. Your workers don't manage procedures, but they do manage the variability that normally arises in conducting work, the little off-normal things that show up in normal work that were not planned for.

We rely on our workers to create success. We can't procedurally control everything, so we hire smart people who can manage problems as the emerge. We count on workers being successful and creating production success and they are good at it. Mostly workers handle small unexpected complications in real time very effectively. Workers essentially complete the system design and work plan. In order to be successful, workers do things that managers aren't able to predict. Workers are quite amazing and are experts at how to conduct their work.

Perhaps the best learning and improvement opportunities in an organization is the ability to immediately tap into the workforce's expertise to discover where your system is strong and effective and where your system is weak and brittle. When we see workers as identifying, prioritizing, and solving problems, we begin to engage our workforce in a different way. The way we see worker roles must change.

A vital shift in thinking is happening in how we view our workers and operators - our workforces. In the traditional view, workers were the problem to be fixed and therefore our "learning" focused on finding circumstances where the worker could be fixed. Finding bad workers was pretty easy and could be done without leaving the conference room. Workers are not the problem to be fixed, workers are the problem solvers to be included in understanding how work is actually done. Shifting from learning what we need to fix our people to learning what needs to be fixed from our workers can be an amazingly powerful change in your organization's future; you will get better at learning.

In reality, when you ask workers what they need to do their work reliably and safely is the workers, they will give you honest answers.

You will get smarter, faster and you will also build trust and credibility within your organization. I caution you that this is more than simply engaging your workforce at the last minute to secure buy-in. You are now in a position to brings workers in early, give them time and space to discover, and engaging them in solution identification. If you have not tried a learning team activity as a learning tool, you will be pleasantly surprised how valuable it will be for your organization. If you use operational learning effectively in your organization, you are well aware of how much information and expertise it will deliver for your operations. As your kids might say, "tap that ship" and get smarter, sooner.[15]

When we use better questions, we get better answers

Effective learning and improvement requires humility by the question asker which forms the foundation for informative answers. The type and quality of questions asked is the ultimate test of your organization's ability or willingness to learn. You can tell a great deal about an organization by looking at the questions that are being asked about operations. Questions are interesting cultural artifacts from which much can be learned.

The questions you ask influence the answers you get. Edgar Schein calls the work he has been doing for the past 60 years in the field of culture, organization, and safety, "Humble Inquiry." "Senior managers always assure they are open," says Schein "and I recognize

---

[15] Edited in the sake of both good taste and acceptability.

that from my culture work. However, what is missing is a climate in which lower-level employees feel safe to bring up issues. In most cultures, speaking up to a person of higher status is taboo. That's why higher-ranking leaders must learn the art of humble inquiry and do the first step in creating a climate of openness. It is their duty as leaders."

Knowing how to find and formulate better questions is a fundamental issue for our organizations' ability to learn and improve. Most people are well intentioned in their quest to make their organization safer and more reliable. The problem does not seem to be in the desire to improve; organizations have a vested interest in getting better. Most organizations do not create strategies to purposefully improve by asking questions in order to learn; organizations usually tend to ask questions in order to confirm what they believe they already know. In a way, organizational improvement is often treated like an accidental benefit. Organizations actually act surprised that their workplace processes and systems get more reliable and that seems really odd to me. After all, it is much easier to learn you are correct in your assumptions than it is to learn the truth about the work being accomplished.

Learning isn't hard. I have made the case that you already pay the world's leading experts in how your facility actually operates. I could also make the case that learning is not difficult or expensive. It means we have to shift our thinking from the belief that workers are the problem to a belief that they are the solution. This is one of the basic tenants of practicing safety differently. All it takes is humility and curiosity about how your organization functions. Leaders have to give up the sense that they already know everything about how work happens; you don't and can't know as much as your workers know.

Learning and Improving from Failure

The third principle challenges us to be deliberate in our learning; learning is vital. Knowing how our operations function, where our operations are resilient and strong or where our operational margins for failure are especially thin is important. We simply need to ask workers relevant questions to discover this important information. We do ask questions to discover this information, I am just not certain our timing for learning is ideal for actual improvement. Most organizations tend to learn from failure, but learning from failure seems too late.

Investigations are extremely important. They are not bad, although they almost always try to describe how a bad thing was not prevented by the organization. We tend to look for circumstances where either the worker or the company were inadequate in stopping the bad outcome from occurring. This search deficiencies that caused failure has not served learning and improving very well. We tend to use investigations to look backwards and desire the ability to change history.

In reality, if we are interested in learning and improving, we want our learning to be directly forward (the future). Instead of fixing the last event, it would seem that we would want to fix all the conditions present that could create the next event. Learning is a vital tool for organizational success that leads to improvement. We must investigate, of that there is no doubt, but our investigations should serve our learning needs first. We really want to learn and explain what conditions existed to create an environment where failure could occur.

An investigation is a learning tool. Investigations promote learning and corrective actions fix conditions. Too often we investigate to quickly address a problem which creates a reduction of both learning outcomes and learning scope. This is true of the concept of "root cause analysis." Root cause analysis is not bad in theory, but it does create some pretty severe operational learning limitations if conducted incorrectly. Organizations tend to "drill down" into an event until the investigation identifies the one main factor that we determine caused the accident. This cause identification is not really based on the event, but more on what the investigation determined the cause to be based upon the investigation that the organization chose to perform. Remember, the question always influences the answer and this is never truer than when an organization does an investigation after the fact.

I am most interested in the fact that when we investigate an event we look at the event in the present time in order to understand the event that occurred in the past in an attempt to learn and improve the organization. Learning is influenced by the bias of retrospect. We are always smarter than the workers who were involved in the event because we know the outcome; the workers didn't have that luxury at the time of the event.

Our investigations (and the tools and processes we use to conduct those investigations) are not the problem. We have many good tools that can be used that are valuable for enhancing learning and helping enact improvement. It seems to me that the timing of learning is the biggest quandary for our organizations. We should shift focus towards a more forward-leaning approach.

Learning from Normal Operations – Learning from Success

All the investigation capacity you have can be used to study normal work as easily as it is used to study failure. The ability to seek potential areas within your organization where failure is probable is an incredibly valuable tool for operational reliability and improvement. We are usually successful and therefore our organizations tend not to recognize success as either special or note-worthy. Because we are mostly successful, we tend to consider utilizing success as unworthy for learning, when, in fact, there is much successful work can teach us.

Erik Hollnagel asked a question the other day that got me thinking about this very idea. Why we are not better at understanding success and the things that keep us successful? Hollnagel asks, "What is happening when nothing bad is happening?" That is an amazing question for the third principle of Human Performance. Imbedded in that question is an important assumption. What does your organization do to manage risk and reliability in real-time in order to be successful? That question can only lead you to a discussion, not about failure, but about the capacity to manage risk. You can see this question changes the way we look at success and really does drive learning. I told you the question was everything; I think this approach proves the importance of asking the right questions.

Learning and Improving is Vital

The third principle of Human Performance is "learning and improving is vital." Vital to what you may ask? Learning and improving is vital to operations and organizational success. Learning and improving is the very essence of operational excellence. Learning and improving is how we grow, mature, and build confidence.

Importantly, the process of learning and improving positions the organization to be better equipped to ascertain real-time operational data. Learning can be messy and it is rather easy to think of ways to speed up the process or simplify it. Don't try to clean up a messy process, for it is in the mess that discovery lives. It is in the messy couplings of your systems, the places where operators feel discomfort, the places where your processes are not strong and robust that the conditions for failure exist. You may not want to know all these details, but you need these details in order to create real and sustainable improvements to your organizational operations. The good news is this information is there for the asking.

Here's a test to see how prepared you are for the third Principle of Human Performance. Let's go back to our three questions:

1. What systems, processes, and tools do you have to openly elicit feedback from your organization, about your organization? How easy to use and available are these tools to every level of your workforce?

2. How open is your organization to actually receiving honest feedback about your operations? How comfortable are you with hearing bad news? Do you embrace the "red areas" and question the "green areas" of your organization? How often do you punish the feedback messengers by, for example, assigning them more work?

3. How committed is your organization to make changes based upon the information you get from your workers? If you ask for feedback (both good and bad) you must also do something with the feedback that you gather; trust is built by making agreements with your workers and then, most importantly, keeping those agreements in a timely manner.

If you can answer these three questions in the affirmative, your organization is moving towards learning and improving as a deliberate strategy.

The data is clear, organizations that are more adept at learning are better organizations. We spend time and money creating improvements in all types of systems, processes, and facilities. Becoming a learning organization is a foundational part of sustainable and deliberate improvement.

Chapter Five

Principle Number Four

Context Drives Behavior

- Workers do what they do for a reason, and the reason makes sense to the worker given the context.
- Complex systems don't lend themselves to traditional metrics.
- Local rationale is information to be discovered, not to be weaponized.
- The environment in which work occurs mainly determines workers' behavior and actions.

Individual behavior is influenced by organizational processes and values.

Organizations are goal-directed and, as such, their processes and values are developed to direct the behavior of the individuals in the organization. The organization mirrors the sum of the ways work is divided into distinct jobs and then coordinated to conduct work and generate deliverables safely and reliably. Management is in the business of directing workers' behaviors. Historically, management of human performance has focused on the "individual error-prone or apathetic workers." Work is achieved, however, within the context of the organizational processes, culture, and management planning and control systems. It is exactly these phenomena that contribute most of the causes of human performance problems and resulting facility events.[16]

---

[16] Excerpt taken from the DOE Standard, Human Performance Improvement Handbook, Volume 1. Concepts and Standards, DOE-HDBK-1028-2009 June 2009.

Workers Don't Get Much Chance to Exercise Free-Will

Let me ask you a question; when you go to the grocery store to pick up a gallon of milk, do you leave the grocery store with only one gallon of milk? It seems to me there would only be two answers to this question: Yes, I get in and then I get out or No, I accidently walked by the cookies which led me to the donuts and I left $100 dollars later without the milk. It doesn't really matter which answer you give to the buying a gallon of milk question, what matters is understanding the relationship between system influences and personal discipline. These two factors always seem to be coupled and, in this example, appear to be opposing forces.

Grocery stores have spent millions of dollars studying shopper behavior. The way a store is laid out has much more to do with the way you purchase items than it has to do with efficiency and effective systems to keep the shelves stocked and make the store easy to manage. Grocery store designers design stores to sell groceries, not to make them easy to manage and operate. The grocery store designer decides it is best for business if the milk is on the farthest wall away from the front entrance to the store. If the milk is a common purchased item, and it is one of the very best sellers, locating the milk in a more difficult location to find exposes the shopper to virtually everything else in the store in route to the milk. When shoppers come in to buy milk those same shoppers will buy other items on the way to finding the milk. The design directly influences sales and therefore profit the store makes selling groceries. This is an example of the store design directly driving shopper behavior. Context drives behavior.

You may think you are in control of your grocery shopping experience. In fact, the store wants you to think you are in charge of this experience, but you are not really in charge of buying only milk. I am amazed by you (and a bit envious) if you are the type of person who said you have the discipline to go in and only buy milk. You are a strong person. I know this because you were in the presence of some powerful system forces that were pushing you, relentlessly, to buy other items. Store design has been studied and defined through years of research and data. The store counts on most of us not having the will power to ignore all the influences surrounding us to entice us to buy more, spend more, and consume more.

There are many examples of how purposeful system design is used to manage and influence behavior. These examples can be found everywhere. Airports, amusement parks, and highways, to name a few, learned a long time ago the way to control behavior is to control the system in which behaviors will occur. I can slow down your driving speed by making the road narrower, restricting your ability to feel like you have a limitless, open road ahead of you. If you feel restricted by the system you behave as if you are in a restricted system. I can make you wait 20 minutes to ride a roller coaster and yet make it feel like you got on the ride 10 minutes early by telling you the wait will be a half-hour when my data says the wait is only 20 minutes.

Systems are very powerful. Context is usually a driving-force for behavior. Workers don't typically get to exercise much choice while being surrounded by the organization's systems. We dictate how we want work to occur by how we design systems and processes that manage work. If I want to slow down a process, I can increase how complicated the process is to complete. Systems are not only effective at driving desired behaviors from the human users of the systems, they have over time become very good at influencing the outcomes the organization wants. I will give you a very effective example of a strong system influence via one phrase: "Shoppers also looked at these items..." Amazon has figured out how to leverage both system and peer pressure to get you to at least *think* about purchasing other items. Sadly, this process works too well.

Organizations are Context Creating Entities

Organizations really are context creating entities is worth repeating. Nothing occurs in your organization that is not influenced by the contexts generated within your organization. In many ways your organization is in this strange loop: The organization creates context, context drives your organization's workers behavior, your worker's behavior makes up the front-facing organization that your customers see and experience, which represents your organizational context (repeat!).

Think of context like this. Your organization is perfectly designed to get the behavior it wants; if you want different behavioral outcomes you must first create different design context. Don Norman, in his book *The Design of Everyday Things* talks about the 7 principles of system design. I will adapt these principles for Human Performance use. We design systems and create context via the following truths:

1. Use both knowledge within the organization and knowledge in the mind of the worker. Both types of knowledge exist. There is organizational knowledge (policies, procedures, work instructions) and there is worker knowledge (machine 3 is slow, the power on line 7 is touchy) and these collectively create your organization's body of knowledge.
2. Simplify the structure of tasks. Make it easy to do the job right and difficult to do the job wrong.
3. Make things visible: create division between execution and evaluation. Remember, the solution for operational complexity is ALWAYS transparency. Make the obscure parts of your system visible. Workers need to know why we do the things we do.
4. Get the mappings correct. Know what you don't know. Ask workers how the work is really done and then ask them to show you how they do the work.
5. Exploit the power of constraints. Know that context drives behavior and think of controls **not** in a hierarchy, as if one were better than the other, but as soft or hard constraints that have the ability to influence behavioral outcomes.
6. Design for error. Do I need to say more? Bad systems expect perfect people and bad systems fail. Work diligently to avoid single-point failure modalities.

7. When all else fails, standardize. Remember the power of process safety and the ability to design safety into your organization.[17]

It is easy to think about the design of systems when thinking about the Principles of Human Performance. Context is a product of the organization's systems and designs. Context is a driving force for behavioral outcomes. Therefore, context has a very significant influence over the behaviors we see in our organizations. Context is not an accident; context is a purposeful part of how our organizations do their essential work, are safe and reliable, and are productive.

We Made it Seem as Easy as ABC

I have been in a constant battle with a rather interesting and powerful safety model; the ABC model. ABC stands for Antecedent, Behavior, Consequence. The model is attributed, loosely and most recently, to Aubrey Daniels. ABC is short hand for human behavior explanation. Aubrey Daniels describes the power and simplicity of positive reinforcement. First, he describes the ABC theory (Antecedent, Behavior, Consequence), which forms the basis for his change management theory. Positive reinforcement has everything to do with individual consequences and promoting desired behavior. To be able to change behavior, Daniels writes, we need to predefine both the

---

[17] Norman, Donald A. (1990). *The design of everyday things*, New York, Doubleday.

behavior we would want to see in our organization as well as the associated desired consequences.[18]

The ABC model, a rather loose adaption of B.F. Skinner's classic work, seems on the surface to give equal power to all three components, A, B and C. The idea that consequence is driving behavior has merit, however the disregard of the power of the antecedent is starting to attract some attention. I will be blunt about this part of the discussion, I think consequence matters, but I am sure antecedents are much more powerful.

The fourth principle of Human Performance is the statement "Context drives behavior." This should not be a very controversial principle. Science has shown that systems are important to behavioral outcomes. Somehow, however, saying systems have power over worker behavior is a bit "touchy" in safety and reliability circles. This stems from years of training our organizations that worker behavior is a choice. Workers either chose to do work correctly or not.

---

[18] Daniels, A. C. (2000). *Bringing out the Best in People - How to Apply the Astonishing Power of Positive Reinforcement.* New York: McGraw Hill.

The idea that worker behavior drives stable outcomes in our organizational processes is not true and runs counter to academic and scientific understanding of system design and context. Thinking workers choose to be safe or unsafe makes safety less of an organizational problem and more of an

> "Accidents are a systemic by-product of people and organizations trying to pursue success with imperfect knowledge and under pressure of other resource restraints (scarcity, competition, time limits)." Sidney Dekker
>
> **Events are System Outputs**

individual problem. This last comment may help us understand why "safety as a choice" has become mythically powerful. It directly questions some very established thinking around your organization, including behavior-based safety concepts.

Behavior-based safety (BBS) programs assume the worker has unlimited power and remarkable self-discipline to make safe decisions. The flip-side of behavior-based safety is the doubt that the organization's context and systems have the ability to influence worker actions. The basic tenant of behavior-based safety is that these programs monitor and change the worker's behavior using a rather detailed and elaborate accounting system. I would suggest that grocery stores don't coach your shopping behavior to buy more products. Grocery stores design their systems to get the outcomes they desire. This argument is on-going and tends to make people angry. Suffice it to say that I think the problem with BBS programs is two-fold: They tend to treat the worker as if he or she is the problem and they assume behavior is a choice and good workers make good choices. This seems to ignore the power of context and its influence on behavioral outcomes. My observations indicate BBS downplays the "A" and overplays the "C" in the ABC model.

The idea a worker "chooses" to be safe, or worse yet "chooses" to be unsafe, runs counter to the fundamental theory of system design. Don Norman tells us that the worker's choice is absolutely influenced by the context in which the choice is made. Workers can and do make behavioral decisions, however like buying milk in a grocery store, these decisions are not made without significant system influences. Systems can and do influence workers, usually resulting in positive and effective outcomes. The fourth principle supports the idea that if you create beneficial context, you will produce positive outcomes. Context drives behavior.

Local Rational

When you stumble upon an operational novelty, for example you walk up to a worker standing on the top rung of a ladder, you usually will make a series of quick assumptions about the worker conducting the seemingly risky task. You can (and should) immediately intervene on behalf of the worker, but that is only the beginning of your responsibilities regarding this occurrence. You will also need to understand how this could happen. How could one of your highly-trained and productive workers do something so risky? What could be going on?

Principle Four should guide you to understand the worker you just "caught" on the top of ladder is in the midst of some very powerful and important context. Instead of seeing this event as a failure of worker judgement, ask how this outcome become possible within the organization's systems? How did the worker become involved to a situation where they end up standing on the top rung of a ladder in order to get their work done?

The only way to ask that question is to shift your thinking from asking "who failed" to asking "what failed?" React to the context, not the person. By initiating your response at the system level and ending it at the behavioral level, you learn more about the context earlier in your quest for an explanation of what is occurring.

One of my favorite examples of context involved a meeting I was attending in Washington, DC. The meeting had drifted in to an argument between Human Performance Principles and Behavior-Based Safety Principles and it was not pretty. Emotions were becoming intense and people were taking sides. In the midst of this debate a strong BBS supporter tried to trap me is some type of safety-worse-case-scenario-verbal-judo by bringing up the following story of work gone bad.

> "I have an example of a risky choice. I had a 50-year-old employee who climbed a 6-foot chain link fence to adjust a robot without opening the gate. The robot moved without warning and seriously cut the man's head. He climbed over the

fence to put himself in harm's way! That is a behavioral problem."

"May I ask some additional questions?" I asked the rather animated man who was giving the example.

"Sure, but what more do you need to know?"

"Did the man climb this fence to sleep, eat, smoke, loaf, or have sex?"

"No, he climbed the fence to keep from shutting the line down. The access to the robot was designed to be interlocked. When you enter this high-risk area properly, it is impossible to get hurt by the robot."

"One more question?" I asked again and he nodded, "When did this happen? Was it the end of the day? Were these workers under some deadline?"

"I don't see how that matters" and the man sat down.

When you spend time determining the context of the event you are capturing something called local rationale. Sidney Dekker calls this "getting into the tunnel with the worker." You are simply taking the time to understand the context of the work in order to understand what context is influencing the worker's actions and thoughts. Understanding how a worker conducts work (and their decisions therein) can only be accomplished by seeking to understand the context (getting in the tunnel with the worker) and the responsibility to seek and understand that context belongs to the organization's leaders and managers, not the worker who was caught on the top rung of the ladder or jumped the fence.[19]

Start Safe – End Safe

We are in the business of managing uncertainty to the best of our ability for our organizations. Knowing the context that drives behavior is an advantage for the organization. If your company wants a different outcome, perhaps you should design a different system. The high-risk intersection in your plant will not really improve if you ask people to be more careful. The high-risk plant floor intersection can be rendered safer if you do a traffic study and redesign the intersection. I know that one options, fix the people, is cheaper and faster to implement. I also know the other option, fix the context and redesign the system, is sustainable and effective. Given the chance, I would always default to the more effective solution.

---

[19] I think I remember this story not because the risk the worker took, but for the ability of a 50-year-old man to climb a chain link fence; that is a remarkable accomplishment if you ask me. One thing you will never hear me say is, "let's climb that 6-foot chain link fence."

You can't really manage the unknown, but you can manage the systems that create known controls and barriers that limits failures that have significant consequence. One of the most important lessons that I keep learning is that when we design a system well from the start, the system will be reliable and dependable. When we start system work well and safe, we tend to end well and safe.

Context Drives Behavior

We have made a pretty good case that the most important tool you have to manage success and failure in your organization is understanding and controlling the context in which your workers conduct work. Good systems have the ability to help you manage the uncertain operational outcomes you will always have. Plans, processes, and procedures are all a part of the overall operational context that you manage in your organization. Manage context on purpose. Learn what your system does and does not do for your workers and operators and then consistently monitor your context to identify if you are getting the outcomes you desire. If positive outcomes are not occurring, don't ask "who" is failing, ask "what" is failing. Start by looking at the system to understand worker behavior, not the old school view of first identifying the offending behavior. Most importantly, remember that context drives behavior.

Chapter Six

Principle Number Five

How You Respond to Failure Matters

- You have two choices: Getting better or getting even.
- You can blame and punish or you can learn and improve, but you can't do both.
- You create the feedback system you have.
- Managers shapes how the organization learns by their reaction to failure.
- Every aspect of improvement is contingent upon leadership's deliberate decision to get better.

Events can be avoided through an understanding of the reason mistakes occur and application of the lessons learned from past events (or errors).

Traditionally, improvement in human performance has resulted from corrective actions derived from an analysis of facility events and problem reports—a method that reacts to what happened in the past. Learning from our mistakes and the mistakes of others is reactive—after the fact—but important for continuous improvement. Human performance improvement today requires a combination of both proactive and reactive approaches. Anticipating how an event or error can be prevented is proactive and is a more cost-effective means of preventing events and problems from developing.[20]

---

[20] Excerpt taken from the DOE Standard, Human Performance Improvement Handbook, Volume 1. Concepts and Standards, DOE-HDBK-1028-2009 June 2009.

Before We Start on Principle Five...A Note

I have to admit, I have gone back and forth on the title for the Fifth Human Performance Principle about a dozen times. In the interest of full disclosure, I would title this principle: "How Management Reacts to Failure Matters." I think this specific wording for this principle is strong, predictive, accurate and true. However, I have been open to some pretty honest and constructive input for this book – and this principle is an example of "the wisdom of the group." I have been encouraged to present this principle in a more organizationally inclusive and reflective way. Leadership appears at every level of your organization – and reaction to failure will happen at every level. Suffice it to say, I have decided to make Principle Five more organizational by using the collective "you." Whatever role you have in the organization, how *you* respond to failure matters. Now, ladies and gentlemen, Principle Five.

People Are Watching You!

Everything you do is important to your organization. People are watching you. The people in your organization determine how to move forward after both successful work and how to recover after failure by watching how you as a leader respond to bad and good information. People are watching closely to see what type of information you welcome and what you don't welcome. How you respond matters. Knowing your workers use your reaction as a barometer to how you are going to respond is a weighty leadership responsibility and an important leadership advantage.

You can tell a lot about an organization by the way its leaders act and react to normal work. Ask your leadership team the question I discussed earlier in the book from Erik Hollnagel, "What is happening in your organization when nothing bad is happening?" and then watch and listen carefully to the way your leadership team responds. You will most likely get one of two potential answers:

> The first potential answer, and the one that frightens me the most, occurs when the leadership team responds by talking about complacency and laziness. That response tells me that leaders think safety is based upon an absence of risk and this gives the impression decreased risk leads to improved safety. That is worrisome because it indicates the leadership team sees the workforce as being at the mercy of workplace hazards and risks. The premise that safety improves when risk is low is completely wrong.

> The second potential answer, and this one pleases me the most, is when a leadership team tells you the reason nothing bad is happening is because their systems and their people are performing as planned. This second, more enlightened group understands that risk in the organization has not decreased (and

most likely will not decrease). In fact, your organization is demonstrating increased competency and an enhanced capacity for risk. This leadership team understands that the capacity for successful work matches the level of risk contained within the system. Operational capacity must always match the risk. This second answer sees safety as a normal function of operations and recognizes the presence of capacity via the absence of events.

Leaders that understand the coupling of risk and capacity are leaders that understand their function as leaders when responding to worker feedback matters. Workers are constantly monitoring their actions and reactions to ensure the organization is on the proper course for future success. Knowing your leadership's attitude has an impact on the organization's context and culture isn't shocking, but it is important knowledge to discuss openly and to use wisely. We have discussed earlier in Human Performance Principle Three about the strategic advantage leaders have when they see learning as a deliberate improvement strategy. Leadership response must be purposeful and deliberate just as learning is purposeful and deliberate. We purposely learn to improve; leadership response should be a deliberate improvement strategy. Event response should be deliberate and purposeful as well.

When a leadership team is faced with an important decision, they should consider what's needed for deliberate improvement by utilizing the following question, "When something happens, what response from leadership of this organization will position the organization to acquire the most valuable information and achieve the greatest improvement?" Don't let your response to events be by chance. Your initial approach and interest will set the course for how the event will be considered by the organization and what you will learn and discover from the event. Be purposeful and deliberate and you will be surprised at what a difference this strategy makes in your organization. It sounds easy, and it is easy, but most leadership teams don't consider this approach a potential area for improvement.

The Fifth Principle of Human Performance that is presented in this book is differs from both the original INPO[21] Principle and the original DOE Handbook Principles that appear at the beginning of each chapter. The original principles espoused the value of learning from operational experience and using this knowledge to improve. This is a great idea, but I am not sure utilizing operating experience is a principle. The original principles were mainly silent on leadership's role in creating a safe, stable, and reliable organization. Neglecting the development of new expectations and leadership changes necessary for Human Performance to be successful appears to be a substantial oversite in the original 5 Principles. We amended

---

[21] INPO is the Institute for Nuclear Power Operations. The original Principles of Human Performance used by the US DOE were taken from the INPO Documents. You can see the influence of James Reason, Patrick Hudson, David Woods, and so many others in this early work. Many thanks to Tony Muschara for translating this work for a more applied use of these concepts.

Human Performance Principle 5 to reflect the special role leaders play in creating robust and stable organizations.

This Change is a Change in the way we Lead Operations

We should begin by thinking about how leadership implements the concepts of Human Performance. Human Performance principle implementation is not **for** your workforce. Let me clarify this. The Principles of Human Performance should make sense to your workforce; engaging workers and using Human Performance principles will be greatly appreciated by workers trying as hard as they can to make your processes, rules, systems, and equipment work as best they can in order to be productive and effective. The Principles of Human Performance create a more systematic method to leverage the profound system and operational knowledge that exists about your organization within your workforce. Human Performance allows you to engage your problem solvers (the workers) at all levels of the organization. Human Performance facilitates alignment of workers, systems, and the organization.

Human Performance is not something done to workers. In that sense, Human Performance is not a new way to manage organizational safety and reliability at the sharp end. Human Performance philosophies offer different approaches to manage safety from the blunt end. Leaders are not exposed in hazards like workers are, but they provide substantial influence on the organization's systems. There is no right or wrong way to implement Human Performance.

Human Performance represents a philosophical shift in how you manage safety, production, and reliability.

What Human Performance has to offer leadership is a set of principles, a set of truths that don't tell an organization what to do, but help an organization understand what to avoid doing. Principles are like truths, they are an accurate way to determine the foundational premises of Human Performance thinking. We don't know everything, but we know these 5 principles are consistently woven throughout all our thinking, learning, and actions in order to create deliberate operational stability, reliability, and improvement.

What role should leadership take in directing implementation of a new approach to safety through Human Performance? The answer is Human Performance leadership exists everywhere in the organization from top to bottom and from the sharp to blunt end. Human Performance leadership must exist everywhere in the organization and how you respond to failure matters deeply in communicating leadership's commitment to reliable and stable performance. Leadership can provide an environment where it is safe to fail and learn. Conversely, leadership can also create an organizational environment where the workforce feels they need to hide important and significant operational data from them, never being discussed, analyzed, or utilized to achieve improvement. Leaders can (and sadly often do) create a chilling environment, discouraging the disclosure of "bad news" to leadership. Knowing less about what is wrong within your organization does not make you better or smarter.

Choices Leaders Make – Getting Better or Getting Even

When something happens in your shop, something akin to an operational upset, you have two choices as a leader (this theme will come up again and again). You can use this event to get better or you can use this event to get even. Both are reasonable choices and are within your power and scope as a leader within your organization. Both will produce significant outcomes, but that is where similarities between these two choices ends. The *choice to get better* will give you operational information about your processes and systems within your organization that you can use to improve and the event you just experienced will be seen as an investment in improvement. The *choice to get even* will be emotionally satisfying because you get to punish the perceived guilty. The event punishment will serve as a temporary deterrent moving forward among your workforce (debatable, but possible) and the punishment response will stop the collection and reporting of information about both the event in question and your larger systems and processes. Choosing to punish the offending workers ensures the event will be seen as a cost to operations and production.

The idea that an event can be either an investment towards operational improvement or a cost on production and profit is a very clear and stark reminder that by what means leadership chooses to respond changes the outcome of how the organization will move forward. Not to oversimplify, but as leaders you really do choose by your actions to signal if an event is an investment or a cost. I can't say this enough; your response will have consequences, for good or for bad. Try hard to shift towards positive responses.

Blame and Punish or Learn and Improve, but Not Both

Anytime something occurs in your organization you have two choices: You can blame and punish or learn and improve. The problem is you can't do both. Many leaders struggle with this idea. We have already built the case that how you choose to respond events matters. I have tried to build an additional case that you should respond purposefully towards sustainable improvement. Don't let your response be an emotional reaction, make it a strategic decision. I am telling you that the option to both punish and learn is not possible. Why you may ask? Isn't it possible for me to serve justice and get smarter at the same time?

Here's the answer to that question: No. There are so many other factors like context, culture, communication, trust, accountability, and the chilling effect that causes punishment to influence and impact workers.

Let's agree on a couple of things I know about organizations before I tell you a little story, let's call these agreements a bit of background assumption management:

> **Agreement one:** All reporting is voluntary; even mandatory reporting is really voluntary. I can only tell you what you psychologically accept or hear and tell you the problems I know, which doesn't include the problems others know or the problems

that can only be identified by collective, organizational knowledge. So, the belief that you will receive timely reports and that you will eventually know what is going on in your organization is fantasy. The question is always more powerful than the answer.

Agreement two: The organization has to build acceptance and freedom around the idea that bad news is welcome. The organization has to establish both trust with the workforce and a method by which bad news can be shared in a safe, non-emotional manner. Leaders almost never want to hear the truth when they can hear they are correct. That is a cold thing to say, but honestly how easy have you made it for your workers and operators to tell you the truth? I am amazed at how infrequently leaders actually talk to their workers and operators about work. It is your duty to create an environment where workers want to give you honest, operational feedback. Feedback from your workers isn't about your workers, it is about your leadership team's openness to receive feedback.

> **We see what we expect to see.**
>
> **We see what we have labels and accounting systems to see.**
>
> **We see what we have skills to manage.**

With those two background assumptions in mind, we should be able to make a fairly strong case that as a manager or leaders, you will learn when you have created the "psychologically safe" space for your organization to tell you news you many not want to hear. People will only tell you what you make it safe to tell you – your ability to create an environment where leaders listen is foundational to actually getting the chance to listen. If you are not hearing the truth, it is not that your workers are not telling you the truth. Not hearing the truth is almost entirely coupled to making space for the truth to be told. In other words, it is you – not them.

When an event occurs, you have two choices as to how you will respond, and based upon the above two agreements, the choice you make will have a long-term effect and be important to your organization's path forward.

When something happens in your organization, you can blame and punish or learn and improve, but you can't do both. You must determine what you want to obtain from an event, an investment or additional cost.

> **You Can Learn and Improve**
> **or**
> **You Can Blame and Punish**
>
> **But, You Can't Do Both**

Perhaps a story will illustrate this point in a bit more of an interesting way. I will certainly never forget this story:

> *A couple years ago I was working with a leadership team on the Principles of Human Performance. The site manager had a strong personality and was very opinionated in his beliefs about leadership. This facility struggled with serious events, although their industrial safety program seemed pretty effective. I just spent an entire day on the Fundamentals of*

106

Human Performance with the team and we wrapped up with some final leadership discussion points. I displayed a slide that said, "You can learn and improve or you can blame and punish – but you can't do both."

*Right after the site manager had read the slide that said blame and punish or learn and improve, the strong and opinionated leader decided to tell me that he could, **and often does**, do both. In fact, he told me he was very good at punishing and learning; he knew the right balance. He told me that he had to learn, that was vital to his operations, but he also had to hold people accountable (culpable) in order to keep his people in line, accountability was equally as vital to his operational success – or so he must have thought. He was very insistent and I thought he was a bit angry by the way he responded.*

Here was this site leader surrounded by his management team in a training class about Human Performance and you could see in the faces of all his direct reports that he clearly was not being successful at performing both punishment and learning. The non-verbal communication coming from his team was telling me to be persistent and push back on this outspoken leader. So, I said "they are opposing theories, when you try to punish and learn you are sending conflicting signals and you will not be effective at either." I then went on to say that on a compass, you could go north-east or any other combination of points that are adjacent to each other, but you can never go both directions on opposing poles (north-south). I thought my description was brilliant. The leader just looked at me and told me I was wrong and that in his years of leadership he has learned to do both. We were at an impasse, fortunately it was the end of the day and I ended the class by saying, "let's think on this...see you tomorrow."

Suddenly, a member of the class came to my rescue and said, "Can I translate this idea into more of a local manner?" I said, "Sure!" glad to be rescued in a time of need. The kind gentleman who offered to help told this brief story:

"If you disapprove of your daughter's first boyfriend you will never get to meet the second boyfriend."

And then the kind gentleman sat down and stopped talking. It was pretty quiet in the room, and in a way that little example was like a "microphone drop" in a Rap battle – a few careful words well stated. I said thanks for a great day and good luck with your Human Performance rollout. I left as quickly as I could, but I could feel something change after that man told his little story, only one sentence long, but brilliant. The message seemingly made its way to the site leader; he was quiet, thoughtful, and thanked me for my time. The amazing thing is that very site now has an amazing Human Performance approach to learning. The number of serious events has decreased and the workers are involved in operational learning at all levels of the facility. Their near miss reporting increased and is now commonplace. They are amazing. I heard a couple months later the site leader told his leadership team that he met his daughter's new boyfriend for the first time after that class and he is a fine young man.

You can either learn and improve or blame and punish, you just can't do both. Don't think about the points of a compass when you tell this story, I love that image but I am not sure it is as effective an example as parenting. Think about your daughter's first (and second) boyfriend. You will want to be involved in your daughter's life, just like you want to lead an organization that is constantly and deliberately improving. It really is a simple choice when you think about it.

Embrace the Red and Fear the Green

Your leadership dashboard may be colored with green boxes, does that mean you are safe? What is happening in your organization when all of your process stoplights are green? What is happening when nothing bad is happening?

The dashboard metrics we use to give us a running pulse of our organization's health and productivity is biased towards telling us what is positive, what is green. Telling you about what is going well may be comforting, but is not very informative. You should fear those green boxes, for they are giving you a false sense of stability and safety. Green boxes should make you wonder if everything is fine. How do we ensure our capacity remains contingent upon our risk if all our boxes are green? A green box never stopped a production failure. Green boxes are not helpful, fear them!

Red boxes on the other hand are an amazing gift to your leadership team. A red box tells you there is an opportunity to learn and therefore an opportunity to improve. Red boxes are your friends, embrace the red boxes and fear the green boxes.

One problem is we have created a culture, over time and with pure intentions, that declares the red boxes are bad. In fact, it is a good bet that your people work hard to avoid bringing you red box information. Green boxes are fun to discuss with your leadership team, red boxes are not fun to discuss, not fun at all. Does that mean they are not telling you everything you need to know in order to make informed decisions? Chances are quite high the "green box bias" is affecting the perception you have of your operations. You have to render the red box, not just a warning signal, but an opportunity to talk about your problems and to build resilience into the dashboard discussion. The bottom line is, if something isn't broken, ask why it hasn't broken yet?

How You Respond to Failure, Matters

Every aspect of improvement in your organization is contingent upon a deliberate decision to improve made by your leadership. Improvement is not achieved by accident. Deliberate improvement is a product of the desire, humility, and curiosity your leadership team exhibits. Deliberate improvement is also dependent upon the feedback systems you create and maintain within your organization. Leadership comes with essential responsibilities.

The purpose of the Fifth Principle of Human Performance is to gently remind leaders of their responsibility to create and maintain a robust organizational culture, a culture of learning and improving. There is a lot of pressure to ensure that your workplace reactions elicit the response you need (and want) from your workers and operators. When you encourage workers to speak the truth to leadership, you will suddenly have much more useful information to utilize for organizational improvement.

I figured out a long time ago, my job is to give leadership the best and most accurate operational improvement strategies as possible.

Leadership's role is to use that information to make sound operational decisions and move the organization forward. Here is what I learned, when I gave them useful strategies, they made better organizational decisions, corrective actions actually fixed issues and the organization moved closer to becoming an organization that learns from itself resulting in consistent and deliberate improvement.

How you react to failure matters. Focus on learning. Question the green boxes, know what is working when nothing bad is happening in your operations. Embrace the red boxes and encourage workers to speak the truth. If you can do these things, your job will get easier and your organization will improve and the only cost to implement these changes is courage and commitment. How you respond to failure, matters – a lot. You are being watched; get caught doing things right!

Chapter Seven

Moving to Practice: Using These Principles to Create Organizational Improvement

"Gosh, I hope this helps."

I hope this book helps leaders, managers, and workers readily adapt and use these fundamental ideas in creating amazing, safe, and progressive organizations all over the globe. Discussing "the basics" of organizational and safety improvement is really refreshing. Putting this book together, I was honored to have the opportunity to go back and learn, think, and research these ideas, concepts I have known and used for years, but never really appreciated like we've done by the more in depth discussion we've had within this book. Going back to first principles provides some very strong advantages for people who think about organizations and reliability, that's for sure. When you are faced with uncertainty, always remember to go back to first principles. Knowing where you came from makes a huge difference in knowing where you are going.

Sometimes when you write a book or give a presentation, you wonder what the audience will take away from the time you spend together. This is not a complicated book, and it is not a very academic book[22], or a long book. This book is really about 5 discrete thoughts. Another person probably wouldn't have prolonged a book like this. Leave it to me, if a normal person can say something in 10 minutes, this same message will always take me a half-hour.

These five principles are the building blocks of Human Performance. They have value to all organizational and operational improvement, no matter what or how your organization is trying to improve. Knowing the principles of how humans perform in socio-technical relationships allows your organization to become smarter. Knowing more always makes you smarter. Having a reliable set of operational

---

[22] Sidney Dekker always calls my books wide and shallow, but he means this comment in a good way and I take this comment as a compliment. I am pleased to give the world a little knowledge about a lot of stuff; you can't drown in wide and shallow waters.

parameters to use when you make decisions, create plans, and transform organizations is vital.

The heavy lifting in the creation and formulation of these principles has been done. Other intelligent individuals have walked this journey ahead of us and learned these lessons for our organization's benefit. We get all the value with minimal strain. These principles, when used and understood, save time, effort, and resources, allowing your organization and other organizations learn from each other. Learning from within and from each other is the true definition of operational excellence.

Organizations that have adopted the Principals of Human Performance have experienced revitalization, transformation, and success in their reliability and safety programs. Organizations that use these principles improve, feel better, and perform better. I desire this level of alignment and improvement for any organization at cross-roads between organizational system improvement and maintaining the status quo.

Bob Edwards once said something to me I have not forgotten. "We should make learning easy, because what we are going to learn is often messy." Bob is right; we often learn of operational conflicts and painful aspects of work that are messy, expensive, and difficult. We know, however painful as it may be, it is better to know and understand than

115

not. These principles allow us to apply solid, foundational knowledge without the requirement to fail and learn from failure. We can leverage other's experiences to cause our organizations to get better without blood and tears. Adoption of the 5 Principles of Human Performance makes it easier for organizations to learn what are sometimes very important and messy aspects of their business.

One of the most attractive aspects of Human Performance is how these Principles make sense on a basic and fundamental level. Colleagues, both academic and from the business sector who crafted these principles for us, have made it easier to understand the basic assumptions of reliability and stability in organizations that are constantly managing uncertainty. These principles are not finished products. As we learn and mature, more knowledge and understanding will emerge. You too can add to this body of knowledge that is constantly being built. I can't wait to see what's next.

All these principles have the same positive objective, to shift, guide, and reinforce the way people think about their organizations and their organizational improvement pathway. We develop our operations, organizations, and beliefs to optimize improvement efforts and the work we conduct. These principles help formulate and give permanence to philosophical points of view. They become the building blocks of what we believe, value, and eventually how we act. Principles help us address what we want to occur when we work in a complex and adaptive environment? Our organizations are developed through their collective beliefs. Principles are the foundation of these beliefs upon which organizational culture is built.

Are We Ever Done? Will We Get There?

When I conduct an investigation, one of the ways I know I am nearly finished is when I begin to learn the same things over again. Learning is being repeated when I am starting to understand more fully how conditions were present and aligned in such a way to create the event. At this point, I know I am getting very close to the complete story. Knowing when you can stop learning is often the most difficult aspect in determining the boundary conditions for an event. The same is true for organizational learning and improvement. We have been taught safety and reliability are an outcome to be achieved. There is a belief if we do our jobs well, someday we will produce a safe and reliable system. In reality, safety is not an outcome to manage, but a capacity, like the battery on your mobile phone. You must continually monitor and match the amount of battery charge you have on your phone with how much time you require to complete the call. Mobile phone battery levels are not fixed or permanent, but in fact the power on your mobile phone is a capacity which allows calls to made and received. Just as we match battery level with mobile phone requirements, we must match risk with capacity. Learning how your system performs is key to understanding how to best meet and monitor operational capacity.

Your organization should never stop learning about how work is actually being conducted. Ceasing learning is simply not possible for organizations and their operational leaders. The reasons are two-fold: The first reason for continuous learning is normal work has no beginning, middle, or end. Normal work just continues indefinitely (never ends). The second reason is we must constantly learn about our organizations is that regular work is never "normal." Normal work always includes variability. Believe it or not, your workers and operators never do the same work task twice because work is always subject to variability.

Work never stops and work is never "normal." These ideas would scare an ordinary manager, but an enlightened leader knows the power of continuous learning and improvement. Work is constantly changing, therefore learning must continue. Since conducted work is never the same, we never really know how work is being conducted.

Principles and Operations – Theory and Practice

Taking this opportunity to discuss and write about the 5 Principles of Human Performance has allowed me to think about, not only the details and specifics about how organizations use these principles, but also how principles like these are meant to be utilized. Principles are theories and theories are essential for understanding and describing our world and advancing knowledge in a way that leads us towards improvement. In fact, theory is how most ideas are understood, researched and tested in a scholarly, demonstrative way, and published so this knowledge is available to the rest of the world.

Theory is the representation of an idea. This idea is tested to not prove the theory as true, but, in fact, to disprove all the divergent ways to answer the theory's uncertainties. We can't prove an idea with 100% certainty. Theories cannot be proven beyond a shadow of a doubt, so we tend to disprove all the other concepts that could create the same outcome. Once you have dispelled the counter-theories, you still haven't proven your theory, but in fact you have supported your theory with evidence.

Stay with me, this very basic discussion of the scientific application of theory (apologies to Sir Frances Bacon) is going somewhere, I promise.

This leads me to the understanding and utilization of principles of all types, whether they are safety, resilience, or Human Performance

119

related. It strikes me that principles are like theories in that you can never prove a principle with 100% certainty (there will always be exceptions to the rule). I can, however, strive to support a principle with evidence via normal, applied practice. Principles allow us to support our ideas with the knowledge of what occurs when they are not followed.

Principles have been tested over time and used in real-life applications in order to establish their effectiveness and influence of Human Performance thinking. In a way, the principles are being utilized as a part of a impactful experiment, our work. We collect information that helps support these principles for the future implementation of these theories. We are a piece of a massive laboratory, the collective knowledge of our organizations.

Principles Capture What We Know Is True

One of the most interesting aspects of Human Performance is how much the Principles resonate with organizational leaders. All of us have taught classes where people say, "this is just common sense." We know the Principles of Human Performance must not really be "common sense" because if this were so common wouldn't we see more examples of Human Performance in organizations as a normal course of action? In fact, these Principles are not common knowledge in most organizations, at least until someone like you comes along to help your organization realize how sensible these ideas are. Human Performance resonates with people, offering a vocabulary and a philosophy that makes sense and because these ideas make sense we assume they are already prevalent in our thinking and actions. Sadly, these ideas are not prevalent in most organizations.

It would be easy to deviate our Human Performance philosophy away from a system approach for organizational safety and reliability to a more individual worker intervention approach, which is not beneficial or effective. One example that is incredibly common is for an organization to immediately dive into Human Performance implementation by teaching "error reduction tools" to every worker and operator. This is not a great idea; teaching tools without an issue in which the workers may apply them to is a waste of time. What's worse is on many occasions, after a concerted Human Performance tools roll-out, driven by an event, these tools are often "weaponized" by management by declaring, "Why didn't you use the tools to stop the event before it occurred?" Staying true to the 5 Principles provides some direction and some guidelines to keep your efforts on track and progressing in the correct direction.

The 5 Principles of Human Performance are, in a sense, a repository of the central values of Human Performance. Keeping these principles at the core of our thinking, training, and practices will allow the basic building blocks of this philosophy to help organizations reduce the philosophical drift that is present and predictable for all safety programs. Having these espoused principles keeps us honest and our Human Performance effort on track (moving in the same direction) and successful. These principles provide some operational and philosophical discipline and provide Human Performance structure and validity across all organizations.

Principles Tell Us What *Not* to Do

Let's take one more look at the 5 Principles of Human Performance, this time from a tactical vantage point. What do these principles tell us as leaders about our organization? How do we best use these ideas to create improvement? How can these ideas save lives?

The 5 Principles of Human Performance

1. Error is normal. Even the best makes mistakes.
2. Blame fixes nothing.
3. Learning and Improving is vital. Learning is deliberate.
4. Context influences behavior. Systems drive outcomes.
5. How you respond to failure matters. How leaders act and respond counts.

Principles don't tell us what to do in our organizations. Like the caution applied by supporting theories without evidence, principles allow us to understand what *not* to do in our organizations. The Principles of Human Performance are, in reality, a way to test our organization's philosophy regarding the management of safety and reliability by building a conversation around what we can support when evidence is not (or has not been) effective. These principles don't tell us what to do or not to do, these principles tell us what is true about human beings performing work within our systems. This knowledge is vital to our organizational operations.

As strange as all of this may sound, the Principles of Human Performance don't tell us how to manage safety, they tell us how *not* to manage safety in our organizations in order to be more successful. By knowing what we should not be doing, our organizational leadership will be guided to a better understanding of what these leaders should be doing, and how these leaders should be acting and reacting in order to be more effective leaders and learners.

Most principles, principles in science, law, and leadership, help to provide operational and philosophical guidance. These principles do so by establishing what we know is true and allowing leadership strategies to be built around these truths, often not to support these truths, but to allow us to build systems and responses to avoid the pitfalls the principles embody.

Principles Help Manage Our Future

The more we utilize and understand the basic building blocks of our fields, the more we can assure success in our planning and strategies. It makes sense if we have this body of knowledge we should use this knowledge for organizational improvement. We understand this knowledge is tested and true. We can depend on these principles to provide us predictable outcomes when conducting normal, uncertain operations. The 5 Principles of Human Performance get us close to the elusive "leading data" that we all desire.

We work in complex organizations and we work with very adaptive and competent people every day. The work we conduct is so fast paced and uncertain, we will never be able to accurately predict or know everything that could possibly go wrong. We exist in a world where accidents occur and sometimes things go amiss. There are very few facets of our work that we actually know and fully understand with a couple exceptions, one important exception is the 5 Principles of Human Performance.

We can and should depend upon these five building blocks of Human Performance in our organizations and workplaces to realize tactical and strategic operational advantages. Advantages not only in understanding failure, but more importantly predicting normal, successful work. The type of work that occurs over again, every day. These 5 Principles of Human Performance help guide thinking towards our organization's strength and ability to ensure safe work occurs during normal, day-to-day operations.

I hope our discussion will ensure that these 5 Principles of Human Performance will continue to play a prominent role in organizational safety and reliability programs throughout the world. Respecting and understanding these principles allow for a uniform understanding and practice for what we all try to accomplish, a workplace with the capacity to manage uncertain outcomes, creating and managing a safe place to work. These principles give Human Performance its theory, its depth, and its legitimacy across organizations and industries.

The 5 Principles of Human Performance provide a common ground for practitioners and leaders in the field of workplace safety, resilience, and reliability. These principles hold us together, allowing us to interact, sharing common ideas and language. Most importantly, these fundamental principles make Human Performance, Human Performance. These principles matter because they represent what, at the most basic level we believe to be true.

Here is my wish for you: These 5 Principles of Human Performance will help you and your organization build an enlightened operational philosophy that will serve as a standard for leadership leading to a profitable future. We don't have bad people or bad leaders. We will occasionally have outliers in our organizations, but mostly we have great workers conducting amazing work. People are not the problem and if it is not the people, that leads us tom focus on our systems.

If our workers are doing their best and our leadership is working hard to create success, the problem is probably not workers the leadership. The issues must reside within our current systems and system philosophies, the manner our systems create context, and– how our systems give our organizations the performance outcomes we require.

Use these 5 Principles of Human Performance for a healthy organization. Do exemplary work, save lives and create opportunities. Create systems and context that ensure success, don't just try to prevent things from going awry. Work hard to ensure the first-class work your workers and operators conduct most of the time continues in a manner that allows your organization continues to learn and improve. Get caught doing the best work you can!

Make the world a better place.

About the Author

Todd Conklin spent 25 years at Los Alamos National Laboratory as a Senior Advisor for Organizational and Safety Culture. Los Alamos National Laboratory is one of the world's foremost research and development laboratories; Dr. Conklin has been working on the Human Performance program for the last 25 years of his 35-year career. It is in this fortunate position where he enjoys the best of both the academic world and the world of safety in practice. Conklin holds a Ph.D. in organizational behavior from the University of New Mexico. He speaks all over the world to executives, groups and work teams who are interested in better understanding the relationship between the workers in the field and the organization's systems, processes, and programs. He has brought these systems to major corporations around the world. Conklin practices these ideas not only in his own workplace, but also in the event investigations at other workplaces around the world. Conklin authored several books, including "Pre-Accident Investigations," a best-selling safety book for many years. Conklin defines safety at his workplace like this: "Safety is the ability for workers to be able to do work in a varying and unpredictable world." Conklin lives in Santa Fe, New Mexico and thinks that Human Performance is the most meaningful work he has ever had the opportunity to live and teach.

Printed in Great Britain
by Amazon

28141846R00076